IT'S
IN
GOD'S
HANDS

IT'S
IN
GOD'S
HANDS

*A Story of Perseverance and
Hope After a Son's
Traumatic Brain Injury*

Tim Siegel
Foreword by Drew Brees

Fedd Books
P.O. Box 341973
Austin, TX 78734

www.thefeddagency.com

Published in association with The Fedd Agency, Inc., a literary agency.

Scripture quotations are taken from the Holy Bible, New International Version®, NIV®. Copyright © 1973, 1978, 1984, 2011 by Biblica, Inc.™ Used by permission of Zondervan. All rights reserved worldwide. www.zondervan. com The "NIV" and "New International Version" are trademarks registered in the United States Patent and Trademark Office by Biblica, Inc.™

Original social media posts, blogs, and writing excerpts have been left unedited for authenticity.

ISBN: 978-1-949784-10-7
eISBN: 978-1-949784-11-4

Printed in the United States of America

First Edition 15 14 13 12 11 / 10 9 8 7 6 5 4 3 2

To my wife, Jenny, my three girls, Alex, Kate, and Ellie, and to my boy, Luke.

I hope this book helps families just like ours.

In loving memory of my mother-in-law, Lindy Swetnam.

CONTENTS

FOREWORD
Drew Brees

I love being the quarterback of the New Orleans Saints. Football is a passion of mine, but certainly not my only passion. Family is my number one passion.

I also love to see the smiles on young children's faces when I come in contact with them. Each time I get that opportunity, I hope to make an impression on them they will always remember.

In August of 2015, I was asked to send a video to lift the spirits of a little boy from Lubbock, Texas, who had been seriously injured in a golf cart accident. Little did I know that would lead to so much more.

Since then I have seen Luke at five Saints games over the last three seasons. I know Luke and his dad, Tim, are big Saints fans, and seeing him has lifted my spirits maybe more than I have lifted his. His fight and will and determination have inspired us all. I see it in the videos that Tim sends of his rehab. It is such an honor and privilege to be a small part of what motivates Luke during those sessions.

He is a fighter. He never quits. I am so humbled to be his hero.

My foundation helps children.

Team Luke Hope for Minds supports children after brain injury. It is strengthening to see that they are taking something so tragic, and turning it into something incredibly positive. A support system and resource for those in need.

I look forward to seeing my good luck charm at many more Saints games in the future! Go Team Luke!

DREW BREES
Quarterback of the New Orleans Saints

PROLOGUE

On Tuesday, July 28, 2015, my son was in a senseless golf cart accident, and everything changed. It has been almost four years and those words are still very difficult to write.

What you're about to read is my very real and sometimes raw account of what has been the most hellish time of my fifty-five years on earth. It has also been a time of surprise and wonder, and reaffirmation of the importance of hope and faith. Anyone who knows me will attest to the fact that I love my family and love being a dad more than anything. I thrive on being there for my children, especially my only son, Luke.

There is nothing in the world that can prepare a parent for what comes after hearing the words "there's been an accident" or "he has severe brain damage." There is nothing that could have prepared me to cope. Not for myself, my wife, my daughters, or my extended family and friends. What I instinctively knew was that I had to cope for my son. Relying on my decades of coaching tennis and the unwavering support of friends, I chose to believe this was not the end of the road. Luke is strong and strong-minded. He would fight if we gave him the chance. It became my mission to find all the ways that would help my boy get better. Throughout the book, I have included some of my Facebook posts from the last four years to relay memories of Luke and to give a glimpse into what was going on at the time and where I was at in the journey.

For the first year or two, I was laser focused on Luke's recovery. Every waking moment was consumed by it. Sometimes at the expense of everyone else. I was in pain, sad, depressed, and angry. And so was everyone else in my family, and sometimes I was too hurt, numb, or scared to see it clearly. But underneath that ugliness and messiness of the struggle to survive our collective trauma was compassion, concern, and love. We were surrounded by a loving, caring community of people. We were blessed with an exceptional team of doctors, nurses, and therapists. And no one has better friends than we do. Love always triumphs. It was the love for my family—my wife, my daughters, and my son—and for other families in our same situation that helped me refocus my energy and efforts, and ultimately find my reason to keep moving forward. To be a vehicle for spreading hope and faith. To impact the lives of others, which we're doing through our nonprofit, Team Luke Hope for Minds.

I share details on the treatment options my wife, Jenny, and I chose for our son. The purpose for sharing is to help people know that there are so many opportunities available to you, to encourage families not to take your diagnosis lying down. Challenge, research, connect with others, do what's best for your child and family. I am neither a medical professional nor an expert on brain trauma or the various therapies and treatments for brain trauma. (My expertise lies in coaching tennis and New Orleans Saints football.) The options my family selected were based on the advice and counsel of Luke's amazing, trusted team of doctors and therapists. I caution anyone against following our course, or any of the treatments mentioned in this book, without the advice and direction of your own medical professionals.

I am not an expert on public safety, or child safety for that matter. I am a father who wants to ensure that there are common-sense traffic laws and guidelines that protect our children from harm. I will unapologetically continue to raise awareness and push for change in my community and beyond.

- For information on brain trauma and treatments, visit: biausa.org
- For information on golf cart laws in your state, visit: golfcartresource.com/golf-cart-state-laws-regulations
- For more information on Team Luke Hope for Minds, visit: teamlukehopeforminds.org

one

MY BOY

It was two in the afternoon, and I was in the middle of teaching a tennis lesson when my phone rang. I answered with a quick hello.

"Luke has been in an accident."

"That's funny, how are y'all doing?" I replied.

"Covenant," the caller replied calmly.

"Seriously, what are y'all up to?"

"No Tim, he's been in an accident."

"You're not kidding?" I started to panic. "How bad is it? Is Luke ok?"

"I think he broke his nose," the caller said.

I ran out of Cooper High School's tennis courts, yelling to my assistant that Luke had been in an accident. I sped down Woodrow Road, and then on Indiana Avenue. As I headed towards 114th Street, I felt a strange calmness come over me. I turned off Quaker, I noticed someone waving frantically for me to turn left. When I did, I saw emergency vehicles near a big empty lot. I slammed on the breaks, jumped out, and ran towards the ambulance where Luke was. A fireman stopped me and said, "Coach, just go to UMC."

"That's my boy! Is he ok?"

He said again to go to UMC, the University Medical Center in Lubbock, Texas. I ran back to the car, and only then noticed the helicopter hovering above. I wondered why they didn't land in the big lot and take Luke in the helicopter. Why was a helicopter there for a broken nose?

As I put the car in drive, I wondered why they were taking Luke to UMC and not Covenant? Something was very wrong, and I had no answers. I arrived at the emergency room at UMC, yelling, "where is Luke Siegel?" to whomever heard me. I saw my wife, Jenny, and ran over to her. She was in tears.

"I think it's bad," she said, sobbing. "And why is Luke here? I went to Covenant, and they told me Luke was here at UMC."

I went near the room where Luke was. There were so many people surrounding him.

Friends began pouring out into the hallway. There was chaos everywhere. I needed to be by myself for a minute, so I walked down the hall, paced back and forth, saying over and over again, "You're my boy, right?"

I said those words to Luke every day. Multiple times a day. I would say it in the car, at home, at practice, from one minute to the next. Sometimes, from one red light to the next. And every single time Luke replied "sure" or "yes." Always in a loving tone.

Saying those words now made me feel like I was talking to Luke and it calmed me down. After I walked back to join Jenny, one of the ER physicians took us into a private room, saying, "I need to talk to both of you alone." Jenny and I closed the door to the room. I knew what we were about to hear was not going to be good.

He looked at both of us with sympathetic eyes and said, "Luke was in cardiac arrest for seven minutes."

I didn't hear anything else he said.

Tim Siegel, 8/30/18

Yesterday evening as I was driving from our hotel to our support group, a song came on the radio that made me think. It was the beautiful song, "Father and Son," from Cat Stevens. Father and Son . . . Luke and I. All at once, memories of us began to hit me. The good times. Father and son bonding. Talks in the car. Throwing balls at each other at Toys R Us. Holding Luke's hand as we found our seats in the Superdome. High-fiving Saints fans outside Cowboys stadium. Laying in bed watching the Rangers, eating cereal together before school while watching Sportscenter. Watching Tech basketball and baseball games. Playing football with his buddies at halftime of Tech football. Picking out his clothes before school. Watching him play

Madden in the basement. Analyzing the Saints playoff chances. These memories kept popping up in my mind. One by one. I kept drifting back to the good times. You know what stopped me from daydreaming? Luke cried out while sitting at a red light. Ironic that the Luke today made a sound while I was thinking about the Luke from before. Father and Son. Almost all of the things I thought of we can still do together. And I don't take that for granted. Nothing stronger than the bond between a father and his son. Especially ours.

I imagine there are many fathers, probably most, who are happy to have survived their son's terrible twos and threes. And the all-boy, messy, and argumentative sevens and eights. Well, I'm not one of those dads. From day one, Luke was the most mild-mannered little boy I have ever met. He loved to please me and Jenny. He was always easy-going, sweet, caring, and thoughtful, except when his sisters got under his skin.

He is the kid who suggested that we drive to a certain spot in Lubbock so that we could give money to the man selling newspapers every Sunday. He was a good friend. I have never seen him argue with one of his friends. Never.

Not too long before the accident, a woman had told me that she knew Luke had a lot of friends, but that he had such a special way of making each of them feel like they were his best friend. It was the ultimate compliment for a father to hear.

More recently, Luke's long-time friend Colton told us that when the boys were in third grade, he never played football with the rest of the kids at recess. He wasn't confident in his abilities, so he had just walked around and watched the other boys play football. He said one day Luke asked him to join the guys. He was unsure, but Luke told him, "don't worry, I'll teach you the game." From then on, Colton played football at recess, and eventually became the quarterback. Today, Colton plays on his seventh-grade school team and credits Luke for his love of the game.

Luke loved having his friends around, sleepovers at their house or ours. I so thoroughly enjoyed hanging out with Luke and his buddies. Luke was just a wonderful little boy to his parents, his friends, his teachers, and to his coaches. He genuinely loved to play ball, especially baseball. He loved to practice throwing, catching, and hitting ground balls every day. You can't say that about many kids his age. He has a strong passion for the game and he worked hard. By the time he was nine years old, Luke had developed into one of the best second baseman around. He respected his coaches and teammates. He wanted to win, but he also wanted his teammates to succeed. The team was always first for Luke.

Every morning, Luke would ask about the weather. If the temperature was over forty degrees, there would be recess. And he would have to wear shorts, so he could run fast. I once drove by the school so I could watch him play at recess. Luke was smiling, high-fiving kids, running around, throwing, catching, loving life. It was a beautiful moment, a glimpse into Luke's life. At home that evening, I told Jenny what I'd witnessed and how impressed I was with his interactions with other kids, and his overall excitement when someone made a good play—even on the other team. "Jenny, I love the way Luke is around his buddies. He is different than most kids. I think he will impact a lot of people in his life." I was sure of it. I had no idea how, or how soon it would come to be.

Luke was mild-mannered and a little shy—the opposite of me when I was a kid. And yet he was competitive in everything: Xbox, recess, or just playing out in the backyard. He didn't want to disappoint, and he didn't like to lose. But if he did, once the game was over, he let it go—also opposite of me.

When Luke was seven, his team was playing in a big game against their rival team. Luke was playing second base. The game was tied in the last inning. There was a runner on third with two outs. The groundball was hit right to Luke, he picked it up and threw it to the first baseman. But it ended up taking the first baseman off the bag, and the winning run scored. His team lost. We walked to the car in silence. After he was buckled in, he said, "Dad, I lost us the game." I told him one play didn't determine the outcome of a game. I reminded him of his great plays. He paused and said, "Love you dad, can we get some ice cream?" Priceless.

Tim Siegel, 12/19/17

3 years ago, Ellie and Luke made their college football bowl predictions. Luke laughed at Ellie's picks. With just a few bowl games left, Ellie had gotten more right. Luke came up to me and said, "Dad is it ok if I change a few of my picks? I just can't lose to Ellie." I said sure buddy. And he smiled and asked if we could go throw the ball.

I remember when Jenny and I found out that we were going to have a boy. I began to dream about all the things we would do together. You see, I am a sports fanatic. I follow every sport religiously. So, it was without question that I would share sports with my son. My friends all joked that maybe my son would hate sports, or wouldn't follow them the way I do.

They were wrong. As early as I can remember, Luke and I talked sports. We had the most unbelievable bond, and sports was our thing. When Luke was three or four, I bought him little NFL helmets and challenged him to memorize all thirty-two teams by the next day. A couple of hours later, he came into my room with a big grin—he had learned them all. I was amazed.

Luke was my shadow, my mini-me. If we weren't playing ball, we were watching it on TV or talking about it. I watched every pitch when he played baseball on the Wii. We watched the Saints beat the Cowboys on Xbox.

I'm from New Orleans. By law that means I am a New Orleans Saints fan. And there is no bigger Saints fan in the world than me. Growing up, it was all about our beloved Saints. By the time Luke was six, it was the same for him. The wins made Luke so happy, and the losses sometimes brought tears. The Saints quarterback, Drew Brees, is his hero. Whenever we played ball in the yard and the park, we pretended to be Brees and running back Darren Sproles, or Brees and wide receiver Marques Colston. The most memorable days are of Luke and I watching our Saints in the Superdome. We made a pact to go to New Orleans every year to watch the Saints, and we went when Luke was six, seven, and eight years old. It was so special—father and son cheering on our team, the same way me and my dad used to cheer on the Saints at the old Tulane Stadium.

As residents of Lubbock and because I coached there, Luke and I were proud Texas Tech fans. We enjoyed watching all the collegiate sporting events. We went to as many games as we could for the men's and women's teams. Luke had a fanbase of his own and was invited to throw out the first pitch at the Texas Tech vs. Texas baseball game when he was six. Luke loved meeting and interacting with the athletes. My office overlooked the football stadium, and after a game the players passed by on their way to their football building. Luke would put his hand out and high-five every player.

We followed the Texas Rangers religiously and watched

every game. Even when Jenny sent Luke to bed, we would watch games in his room until he fell asleep.

Just like we did two nights before the accident.

Dear Luke,

It's your birthday. You are 12 years old today. You had 2 hours of therapy and slept right through it. As a matter of fact, you didn't wake up until 5 p.m. today. You loved your birthday because you got the opportunity to have people spend the night. You loved having friends over, and you really loved spending the night with your buddies. Today we would have thrown the football and baseball. Maybe we would have gone on a bike ride. You and I would ride side-by-side, singing "Out in the Street," by Bruce Springsteen. I would sing "out in the street," and you would sing "oh oh oh oh." Then of course we would switch channels from the NBA playoffs, to the NHL playoffs, to baseball. Mom would tell me to get you to bed, and we would smile at each other because we knew that I would turn the TV on, so that we could watch a little more. Before you would fall asleep, your Under Armour clothes would be laid out. When you woke up—and we knew when you woke up—you would sneeze, as you did every morning. Your first words to me were "can I have some cereal on the couch, so I can watch Sportscenter's Top 10?" Then you would tell me that you were excited about football at recess. We listened to music on the way to school, usually "The Saints are Coming" by U2 and Green Day. As I dropped you off at school, you and Ellie would walk towards the door . . . and every time you would turn back and wave at me. I couldn't wait to talk to you after school. And when you had baseball practice, I was as excited as you were. I loved watching you interact with your teammates, and I especially loved how you always gave 100%. When Texas Tech had a sporting event, you were always by my side. I miss all of that. I miss talking about our favorite athletes. I miss it when you wanted me to watch you play Xbox. Cowboys vs. Saints. I miss when I would lose a tough match at Texas Tech, and you would look at me with sad eyes, and say "sorry Dad." You know what is so crazy? I told your mom that you were going to impact a lot of people just a few months before your accident. I saw how you cared about others. Well, little buddy you are impacting so many people. You will always be my boy I am so proud of you. I love your fight. I love when you move your tongue when I talk about your friends, Drew Brees, or if you want some frozen lemonade. You WILL get better. God is with you. Your family is with you. And friends in Lubbock, and all over the world are praying for you every day. I love you Luke. You're my boy right? I can't wait till the day you say "sure Dad." Just like you used to.

two

UMC

I heard the words "cardiac arrest" and just lost it. I banged my hands against the wall over and over. What happened next isn't quite clear. What I do remember is that my hands went numb, then my feet and my face. I asked my daughter Alex to get my phone out of my pocket. I don't remember when she came into the room.

"What is happening to me," I remember asking myself. A nurse looked at me and rather sternly said, "You have to get it together. Your son needs you."

I remember I could hardly breath. The next thing I knew, I was sitting in a wheelchair with an oxygen mask on my face. I have no idea how long that whole episode lasted. It could have been minutes, or more than an hour. Alex later told me I asked her to make some calls for me. I have no recollection of that conversation.

Tim Siegel, 6/28/18

"Don't look back." A friend told me this last weekend. Another friend sent me a text that said, "it's not what you are running from, it's what you are running to." Yesterday on Facebook, I saw a quote from George Strait, "If you don't leave the past in the past, it will destroy your future. Look what's in front of you, not what yesterday took away. The best is yet to come." These are so good for me to read, and I imagine it is for all of us. I can't tell you how difficult it is for me not to look back. I fight it every day. Some days I win, other days I get knocked out. I know there is a distinct difference between looking back with sadness, and looking back at great memories. But that line gets blurred very easily. For me, they tend to be one and the same. Last night during our support group, I looked around at all of the parents who are caretakers for their child. And I remember thinking how much I admire them for their commitment and dedication to their sons. At that same time, Randall Williams, our PT and speaker, said that we do more for him than he does for us. All of us in that room have a responsibility to look forward, to run to something, and to not let the past destroy our future. For our entire family. Today, this beautiful family came from Austin for therapy for their little girl. My heart was full watching her give all she had to try to walk. And to see the enthusiasm from the therapists was wonderful. Please pray for my little hero. His tummy has been bothering him, as having regular bowel movements is rarely a given. I chose this video from Tuesday because Luke was so alert. He is listening to my every word.

Luke was eventually moved upstairs to the ICU, to room 245. Jenny and I were taken to the family suite reserved for the families of the hospital's most critical patients. For a while, I sat on the window ledge overlooking the courtyard, and I prayed. I asked God to protect Luke, and to give Jenny and me strength.

There was a door between our family room and the ICU waiting area. I peeked through the window and saw at least fifty people in the waiting area. The mood out there was far different than our room. They were out there smiling, laughing, talking loudly. How was that possible? This was the darkest moment of my life. I felt so alone, helpless, and in shock. I was peeking out at a world that didn't exist for me anymore.

Word had spread quickly that Luke was in an accident. My phone was pinging nonstop with message after message after message. Comments were posted on Twitter, and it made the local news. That first evening, visitors came and went—over a hundred people at least. Jenny's friends, my friends, Texas Tech coaches and staff, Luke's baseball team, Kate's basketball team, Ellie's cheer team, and so many others. Everyone wanted to be there for Luke and for us, to offer prayers and support.

Jenny and I didn't sleep that first night. I sat on the couch, I paced the room, I visited with friends, and I sat with Luke. I watched as his big sister Alex held his hand as they both slept. It was a precious, beautiful moment. But gut-wrenching. Mostly though, I walked the halls by myself, still whispering "you're my boy, right" again and again. I felt all alone and frightened.

We made it through that first night, and even the second day. I honestly don't know how, and I barely remember it. The third day, July 30, 2015, was a blur of machines, doctors, nurses, and visitors. The doctors were being hyper-vigilant about his brain pressure, heart rate, and blood pressure. I listened to their every word. I watched them for tell-tale signs, indications of Luke's prognosis and progress. *What were they really thinking? How bad is it? Was he going to survive?* I started watching the numbers on the machines, having figured out what they were reacting to. Whenever his brain pressure numbers went up, so did my heart rate. That's the number they were paying extra close attention to.

The waiting room was still packed. The four first responders came by to check on Luke, and so did the young man who was the first one there to help Luke. He had been working in a yard across the street from the accident.

For some reason, it made me feel better to be out in the waiting area with everyone. Or maybe I could fake it better by not having to face my fears right away. It also helped pass the time. I wanted time to go by faster; I just wanted to get past seventy-two hours.

The doctors gave me little optimism. I could sense their concern. But there was no way Luke was going to die. *No way God, please no way.* If he didn't survive, neither would I. Deep down I sensed that.

Then there was the MRI, and we finally knew. Luke had severe brain damage.

• • •

At the end of our first week at UMC, I met a woman whose daughter was recovering from an ATV accident that had happened a year earlier. She wanted to encourage us, give us hope. She was so thoughtful to visit and spend time with us. But that night, my nine-year-old son underwent surgery to repair skull and facial fractures. Hope was elusive.

The month of August was hell. There's no other way to describe it. I was not in a good place, mentally or physically. I felt useless and that everything was out of my control. The stress was high. Not surprising, I relied on my athletic training to get me through the bad days. I challenged myself to do 103 push-ups and 303 sit-ups every day to keep my heart strong and the stress manageable. The number three holds special meaning in our family, and was Luke's favorite number.

Each day brought a new worry, a new stress, a new mountain to climb. Our seventh day at UMC, August 3, should have been my first day of tennis practice at Cooper High School. Instead, I was here monitoring machines, praying my son was going to wake up. Our frustration levels were chart-topping. Our emotions, all over the place. It annoyed Jenny that I spent so much time in the waiting room instead of being in Luke's room. I was sometimes rude to the nurses. We were both exhausted and unable to eat.

We would wake up to high brain pressure numbers, well above the desired "below twenty" range. The morning of August 4, Luke's brain pressure was extremely high, and Dr. Belirgen, one of Luke's physicians, performed an EV (external ventricular) drain to relieve the pressure. But his brain pressure continued to rise. Higher and higher. The EV drain hadn't helped. Luke would need another surgery, a craniectomy, to remove his skull.

The surgery was at 6:00 p.m., but by midnight, his brain pressure had shot up again. By this time, I was close to losing my mind. At 1:30 a.m., Luke went back for a third surgery—a duraplasty—where the dura, the brain's cover, is cut open to expand the dural surface. I asked our neurosurgeon what our options were if this didn't work. "We are out of options," he replied.

Around 3:00 a.m., Luke was taken to room 234, a new, more spacious room that hopefully would bring a new vibe and better results. I waited outside Luke's room because I was afraid to see the numbers. But they kept rising . . . fifteen, twenty, twenty-two, twenty-four. *Oh my God, no!* I slumped against the wall. Then suddenly they dropped, and kept dropping, and hovered between six and ten. I sat on the floor, still leaning against the wall, looked up and thanked God.

After a few minutes, I approached Dr. Belirgen to ask him what he thought of the situation. He looked me in the eyes and quietly whispered, "I don't know if Luke is brain dead. We don't know yet." It was now 4:30 a.m., and I began pacing the halls again thinking of the worst. I began to rehearse a speech for Luke's funeral.

Around 3:00 p.m. the next day, Wednesday August 5, my world changed again. Dr. Tiva, Luke's intensivist and a critical care physician, came to play his ukulele for Luke. I had mentioned before how much Luke loved music. While Dr. Tiva sang and played "Stand by Me," the monitor showed squiggly lines. Squiggly lines meant there was brain activity! I was witnessing a miracle. Total desperation and defeat turned into victory and joy in a matter of two seconds.

In the middle of that excitement, two Texas Tech colleagues and friends had come to visit us, Tyson Carter, the men's tennis strength and conditioning coach, and Todd Petty, the women's tennis coach. I was on a high, I grabbed Tyson and Todd and went outside to throw the football. It's probably not the reaction you would expect, but it was my way of relieving stress after being so low for eight days. Looking back, I think it was only fitting that I would go out and throw the football. It's what Luke and I did when we wanted to avoid chores or homework.

Tyson and another good friend Jamie Lent spent the night in our family suite that night. Their presence offered a nice change of pace and a little relief from the constant worry. I still woke up every hour to check Luke's brain pressure levels. That night we were spared, and his levels remained in the safe zone. Thank God.

Speaking of friends, it would be impossible to mention everyone who came to visit Luke, Jenny, and me in the hospital. It would require another chapter to properly acknowledge and thank everyone who came by, brought food, and helped with the Pray for Luke shirts and bracelets (which were designed, ordered, and distributed in a matter of days!). I think about Michael Center, my good friend and the tennis coach at Texas, who cut his vacation short and flew in from Colorado to visit Luke. Michael's support has been unwavering. He has been there for me ever since the accident. I think about Bobby, Simon, Tyson, Todd, and countless others who spent hours upon hours consoling, counseling, praying, entertaining us—feeding our bodies and our spirits. I've had friends tell me it was good for them to see Luke in the hospital. My response quite often was, "you were there?" During those first weeks, I was in such a fog, and the whole ordeal felt like an out-of-body experience. We had such an outpouring of love and support. And the hope that Dr. Pinkney gave us each and every day helped us tremendously. And for that I am so appreciative.

The next several days were a mix of highs and lows. We had to process new health concerns for Luke, and the emotional well-being of our young daughters Kate and

Ellie, ages twelve and ten. We arranged for both of them to get counseling. We got used to not showering every day. We had to sort through the impact this ordeal was having on our extended family, some of whom were struggling to comprehend the severity of Luke's situation. And we worked hard to be present in the moments that deserved our gratitude.

The day after we saw brain activity on the monitor, Luke's head began swelling. The day after that, there was concern about his lungs. He also opened his right eye that day, but we didn't know if he could see and if it was a moment to celebrate. However, the next day, August 8, was an optimistic, uplifting day. Luke was exhibiting signs that he was trying to wake up. Some of the Texas Tech athletes brought signed posters for Luke's room. First responders came to visit. And a friend brought Luke a helmet autographed by Drew Brees. A friend of ours, Courtney Davis, set up a GoFundMe campaign to raise funds for Luke's care. Local papers were still covering Luke's accident and progress. All in all, the support from the Lubbock community, and beyond, was amazing.

• • •

A couple of days later, Luke experienced neurostorming, a nervous system disorder, which made his heart rate (and mine) incredibly high. Dr. Belirgen told us not to lose hope. That was followed by surgery to treat a bleeding ulcer, and then unsuccessful efforts to get Luke to breathe on his own. In the end, his jaw was too weak, making it difficult to extubate, or remove the breathing tube.

On August 14, Luke had three surgeries: a tracheostomy to insert a breathing tube; a procedure to insert a gastrostomy (feeding) tube, and a craniotomy to remove a bone flap from his skull to relieve his brain pressure. Sores had developed in Luke's mouth and on his tongue, and the doctors advised that the trach would help. After the surgeries, Luke's brain pressure spiked to thirty-eight then returned to normal. He developed an infection and his temperature spiked to 103.7. All we could do was pray that the antibiotics did their job.

I don't know how I survived that week.

Shortly after, Jenny and I started sleeping in Luke's room, instead of the family suite. I think we got even less sleep. One particularly rough night, his breathing tube had to be suctioned every fifteen minutes, and I finally fell asleep at 4:30 in the morning. The next day, one of his wounds started leaking, resulting in yet another surgical procedure—his ninth in one month.

Over the next two weeks, we tried to bring back a sense of normalcy to our lives, for the girls' sake. We started with little things, like going home to shower and to play with our cockapoo, Saint. Jenny attended an open house at the kids' elementary school, Cooper Central. I'm sure I will never fully comprehend how difficult that was for her. I spent a night at home with the girls, finally. And Jenny did the same a couple nights later. By that point, we had spent an entire month at UMC.

Towards the end of August, Luke's condition seemed to have stabilized, and the doctors moved him out of ICU to pediatrics. We immediately missed the nurses and the constant hands-on care of the ICU. Jenny was now Luke's full-time nurse, in a matter of speaking. A few days after the transfer, Jenny noticed that Luke's pupils were dilated and his eyes were twitching fast. She demanded an MRI, and Luke got one. The test showed that Luke had had a seizure. Dr. Belirgen performed a lumbar puncture, or spinal tap, to remove built-up fluid. Luke's tenth procedure.

Jenny and I decided to go home together that evening. It had been a long, hard day, in a series of long, hard days. We both needed a break and some time to decompress a bit. A friend of ours stayed with Luke because we were adamant that he not be left alone. When we got home, Jenny went to Luke's room, which is where I found her crying hysterically. It will always be one of my saddest memories. Seeing my wife filled with grief and pain, pouring out her heart. There was little I could do. I just held her and guided her to our room. Then I uttered a simple prayer: *Oh, my God, help us.*

September was off to a good start, all things considered. On September 3, we learned that Luke had been accepted to Cook Children's in Fort Worth. Cook Children's is a very well-respected medical center in Fort Worth, Texas. This was great news for Luke's long-term treatment and recovery. He was going to be transferred on September 10. The day before, we got to bring our dog Saint to the hospital to visit Luke.

After forty-four days, our time at UMC had come to an end. Jenny, who hates to fly, would travel with Luke on the medical plane. Her sacrifice knows no end. I would follow by car. The day of the move, we arrived at the hospital, packed up Luke's belongings, and began our walk to the ambulance that would transport Luke to the airfield. What happened next was unbelievable.

As we entered the first floor, nurses, doctors, staff were lined up on both sides of the hall clapping and cheering for Luke. Over seventy-five people had come to see him off! It was quite an emotional scene, and we always be grateful for how they cared for Luke, and for us.

At the airfield, I sat on the edge of the runway watching the plane prepare for takeoff. As it lifted off the ground, I dropped to my knees and sobbed like a baby. All the emotions I bottled up the last forty-four days poured out of me.

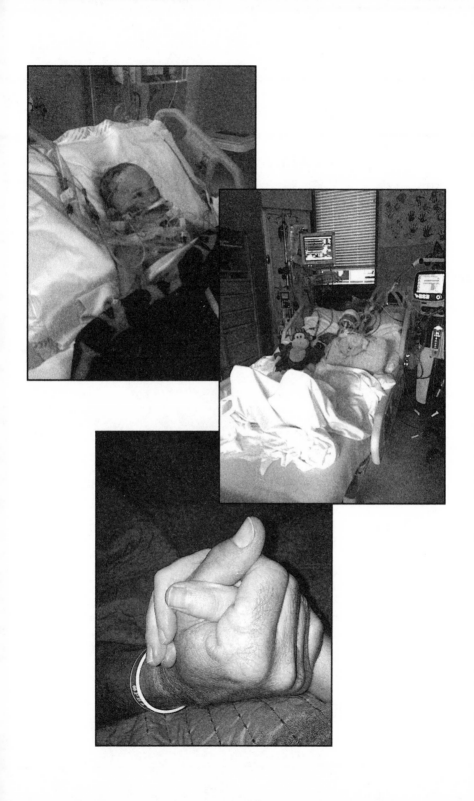

three

COOK CHILDREN'S

My son was being flown by medical flight to a hospital in Fort Worth. It didn't seem real. I tried to get up, but I felt paralyzed. Eventually, I managed to get in the car and drive. Halfway into the trip, I pulled over and took a twenty-minute nap. The stress and emotional toll had absolutely drained me.

As I turned off at the exit for Cook Children's Hospital, my stomach churned and my heart raced. I parked and made my way inside. I took the elevator to the fourth floor, neurology. I was met by Laura, a secretary who realized right away I was Luke's dad. Jenny was waiting for me with tears in her eyes. She felt good about the nurses and staff she had met.

Jenny and I had decided that she would stay with Luke, and I would return home to take care of the girls and to coach the middle school and high school tennis teams, as best I could. I did not want to leave Luke's side, but I had a responsibility and an obligation to return to Laura Bush

Middle and Cooper High. We worked out a plan, with the approval of the school superintendent, Keith Bryant, for me to spend Tuesdays with Luke at Cook. I would leave early morning to drive the four and a half hours to Fort Worth, stay at Cook for four or five hours, then drive back home. I would return on Friday afternoons with the girls, spend two nights and go back home on Sunday evenings. My friend Dave Marcinkowski let us stay in one of his apartments that was just a few miles from the hospital. We were still being supported and blessed by our extended network of friends.

Jenny was impressed by Cook Children's Hospital in those first few days—the friendly staff and all the services and amenities the hospital had to offer patients and their families. There are music rooms, an outdoor play area, a salon, and even a Build-a-Bear Workshop. And, very important to Jenny, a Starbucks. On our fifth day, a meeting was scheduled with the therapy staff, the nurse manager, and our neurosurgeon, Dr. Acosta. Fortunately, September 15 was a Tuesday, so I could attend with Jenny. We were nervous about the meeting but looking forward to their plan for Luke. I knew that the goal was for Luke to do rehab every day, but I didn't think he was physically or mentally capable. I had scoped out the rehab facility and the gym. The kids I saw were in much better shape than Luke. I was concerned. I wondered if Cook Children's was going to be good for Luke. *Was he strong enough to be here? Were they expecting a patient in a better state? Was it too soon?*

Jenny and I walked into a conference room on the fourth floor. As the meeting got started, we felt better right away. The first nurse we met was a Texas Tech alumna, so we had an immediate, strong bond. The Cook team went around the room explaining their treatment plans to help Luke. One by one. They were all professional and positive. When Dr. Acosta began to talk through his plans, he moved his iPad towards us to show us the picture of Luke's MRI. We could finally see just how badly Luke's brain was damaged, globally. He then said words that neither of us had even considered, "Based on his MRI, Luke should never use his voice or his limbs. Ever."

The tears began to flow down Jenny's cheek. Everyone in the room was silent. I was in shock. I felt like I was in a movie. This wasn't real. *Please God tell me this is a bad dream.* Dr. Acosta suggested that everyone give us some time alone in the room. The staff exited, but before they left, I asked Dr. Acosta one question. "Have you ever seen an MRI that bad with more improvement than expected?" He nodded and said yes. They all left. Jenny cried and cried. I just held her.

I experienced a range of emotions the first two weeks at Cook. I began to get angrier and angrier. I attribute it to the time I spent in the car driving back and forth to Fort Worth. It gave me time to think and begin to process what had happened, how our lives had changed. God, I missed my son. He was still with us, of course. But I missed "us," the way we were as father and son.

I also knew this was extremely hard for all three girls, especially the younger, Kate and Ellie. Their life wasn't the same either. Spending every weekend in an apartment in another city and sitting in Luke's hospital room was going to be challenging for them. I felt rage, for the first time in my life.

On Mondays, Wednesdays, and Thursdays, when I was home, I found it impossible to motivate myself to do anything. I could barely sleep, and when I did, I woke up facing our nightmare again and again. Jenny would call from the hospital, and I would act like everything was ok. I lied to her about my day and my moods. I tried hard to be there emotionally and physically for the girls. I would psych myself up as I drove to school to pick them up. I wondered if they could tell how much pain I was in.

I struggled with attending Kate's basketball games. I used to love it, when I was right in the middle of the action with the dads. But not now. I told Kate I couldn't go, but after missing a few games, I promised her I would be there for the next one. As I entered the gym, it felt like all eyes were on me. I took a seat and kept my head down so no one would come up to me. I didn't want to see anyone or talk to anyone that night. Later that night, I sat in Kate's room with tears in my eyes and apologized for how I had been acting. I shared with her that I had been feeling so much pain and that I was struggling to get through the days. She told me that she felt the same, and I realized that I was so consumed with my own emotions that I hadn't been aware of her grieving. My pain was too overwhelming and it was affecting my parenting. Something had to change. I began taking an anti-depressant to try to cope.

The Texas Tech vs. TCU (Texas Christian University) football game was September 25, and I was upset that Luke and I wouldn't be there. It might seem small and irrational, but it was evidence that our happy traditions might be over. It was proof that I needed to start facing reality. It became crystal clear when doctors advised us that

Luke will likely need twenty-four-hour care for the rest of his life. My heart broke into a million pieces.

I made a point to get to know the nurses and the therapists at Cook Children's Hospital. They were amazing and always available. They had gotten used to seeing me in the room, every Tuesday, Saturday, and Sunday, and to answering all my questions. The nurses quickly learned that we are Saints fans—not Cowboy fans—and Texas Tech Red Raider fans. It made for good banter.

It was now October, and not a lot had changed. Luke went to therapy a couple of times a day, but quite often the therapist sent him back to his room because his blood pressure and heart rate were too high. On October 26, he underwent a twelfth procedure, to insert a Baclofen pump to improve his muscle tone.

My emotional and mental state hadn't changed. I still didn't sleep well, and I was full of anxiety and guilt. I carried a tremendous amount of anger, some directed at myself. I became isolated, preferring to lay in bed and watch TV. Every Saturday, I watched Texas Tech football in Luke's room. It wasn't the same, and I grew more depressed. Deep down, I knew that I needed help, so I met with a pastor for counseling.

Jenny went home at the end of October to spend Halloween with Kate and Ellie. I stayed with Luke for two days. For the first time since coming to Cook Children's, it was just me and him. Up to now, Jenny had been hands-on with Luke's care. It was time for me to step in. I learned how to change his trach. I paid close attention to his medications, doses, and reactions. I quickly noticed that Sinemet makes his heart rate go up and, within fifteen minutes, causes him to dry heave for at least five minutes. It was all I could do not to cry. Sinemet is a neurotransmitter, so it's important that Luke take the medication. The doctors said his body needed time to adjust to the drug.

I had hoped the break would give Jenny time to experience "normal" life for a couple of days. I know the girls were happy to have their mom home and were looking forward to a fun Halloween. Our expectations were bigger than our reality. It's difficult to switch between the two worlds we inhabited, and this was Jenny's first attempt in almost two months. She had a miserable time at a Halloween party, especially when she saw kids riding on a golf cart. Being around young kids, especially those Luke's age, is hard. I struggled with it, and Jenny must have too. We want to keep things as normal as possible for Kate and Ellie. They need more of our attention, they need us emotionally. And I for one was doing a poor job.

The day Jenny was supposed to return to Cook, I received a phone call that she was in the hospital. She'd had a panic attack, her second one. She couldn't swallow or breathe. It was clear that she needed a longer break. I asked her to stay at home for two weeks to rest. I felt like I was up to the challenge of caring for Luke on my own.

This wasn't UMC, where I could sit outside and visit with friends. I needed to step up. I would have fifteen straight days with Luke without Jenny's wisdom and oversight. I monitored every dose of medication. I watched every therapy session. I laid next to him in bed. We read together and listened to music. I got to know the fourth-floor staff members, day shift and night shift. All of them. They all loved Luke and were so sweet to him. I gained more respect for them and had more admiration for what they do every single day. They taught me so much: patience, persistence, professionalism, and most of all, a positive attitude.

I also learned so much about myself, including that I was stronger than I realized. I honestly hadn't known if I could handle the highs and lows, although there were so few highs. But I found ways to cope. At times, I would take a walk around the hospital or go outside for a breath of fresh air. I began to turn a corner, emotionally. I was no longer teetering on the edge of a breakdown. For that reason alone, those two weeks with Luke were probably the most important of my life. A God thing?

I observed something on my walks that bothered me. It might sound a little judgmental, but I feel very strongly about it. It amazed me that some of the patients were alone for hours at a time. Sometimes a day or two would go by before I saw anyone. It's such a sad situation. I realize that work or other obligations may prevent parents from spending every waking hour in the room, but arrange to have a friend or family member be there. I feel it is important to have someone present in the room as often as possible—to monitor and advocate for their child, and mostly to make sure they're surrounded by love. My experience in just a few short months is that love is the best medicine, the best therapy, and the best way to recover. For me and for Jenny, we had to be with Luke every single day and night. We were blessed to be able to do it.

Luke's condition had not improved a great deal, and he continued to experience health issues regularly. There was plenty that concerned us and the doctors. At the same time, so much good was happening around him. The Texas Tech volleyball team came to visit Luke when they were in town for a game at TCU. Later that same day, a friend of ours asked his son to come sing for Luke. They had heard that Luke loved music and was huge fan of Ed Sheeran. They brought a guitar and a drum and sang Ed Sheeran's "Photograph." I was worried the noise would be too much for Luke and the other patients on the hall, but when I looked at Luke and then the monitor I didn't care. Luke's heart rate went from 126 to 77. He loved it. It relaxed him. He was enjoying this moment with us.

The next day we had a care meeting with Luke's team. We had them regularly to check on his treatments and progress. That day we were told that Luke would be discharged in four weeks unless he started to show improvement. Cook Children's is a rehab hospital, and Luke's therapy sessions were inconsistent because of frequent blood pressure and heart rate spikes. On a rational level, I understood, but I didn't want to hear it. Give him time, I thought. I didn't want to leave just yet.

I shared this update with my good buddies Michael Center and Kevin O'Shea. They decided to drive out to visit us the next day. We were gathered in Luke's room, when suddenly we heard Luke making sounds over and over. We looked at each other in shock. He used his voice for the first time in almost three months! We were witnessing a miracle. When word got around that Luke had made sounds, many of the nurses ran to his room. There were hugs and tears from everyone. One day before, we had been told Luke needed to show improvement. And now he uses his voice. Definitely a God thing.

Thanksgiving was drastically different this year. Friends volunteered to cook for us and bring food to the hospital. Over the last few months, I had met and gotten to know parents who were in similar situations, experiencing similar pain. We invited them to share Thanksgiving with us. We were in it together.

In early December, my parents came to visit. I could see the toll this ordeal was taking on them, especially on my mom. She's tends to be emotional and a worrier. Every time we talk, she tells me that Luke will talk again, and most of our phone calls now end with her voice cracking. I wasn't sure how seeing Luke in person would affect her. I was sure that Luke's accident would take years off her life. As it had mine.

We were sitting in Luke's room when the main therapist asked me to step out for a chat. She looked serious. Once outside the room, she said: "Luke is going to have to go home next week. He isn't improving enough. It will be good for him at home." I walked back into Luke's room in a daze. I couldn't believe what I had just heard. He had just used his voice a week earlier. We asked if Luke could stay until January, and the doctors and staff said yes. I wasn't ready to go home, and I didn't think Luke was either. I wanted to a few more weeks to give Luke a chance.

On December 14, Luke had a very special visitor: the Texas Rangers' Elvis Andrus. Elvis is Luke's favorite baseball player. I'm convinced Luke knew he was there, because he made sounds the entire time Elvis was in his room. A special thank you to Emily Jones of the Texas Rangers for making Luke's day, as well as mine.

There is a lot to love about Cook Children's. As Christmas approached, they went to great lengths to ensure their families felt the Christmas spirit. The staff set up rooms for children to pick out gifts for their siblings. Absolutely, incredibly thoughtful. On Christmas Day, in room 449, Kate and Ellie got to open Christmas gifts. It was not the Christmas any of us wanted, but Cook Children's and their amazing staff made it one to remember.

Tim Siegel, 12/24/15

Today is day 150. I woke up this morning at 5:00 thinking about quotes from Luke that made me smile. "Dad, I am beginning to understand why the Saints traded Jimmy Graham. We have to get better on defense." "Dad, watch me destroy the Cowboys on Xbox." "Dad, let's watch the whole game. Mom will never know." "Dad, are you sure our new backyard will be big enough to throw long passes?" Dad, don't say no, but can I have someone spend the night?" "Dad, we can't go to school till I watch Sportscenter Top 10." And, of course, watching Luke tear up after a Saints loss made me smile. And there's nothing like watching sports with Luke and out of nowhere he would say, "Dad I love you." I dropped Luke and Ellie off at school every morning. They both would say "Love you Dad," and then walk towards school. Luke every time would take a couple of steps and turn around and wave. Melts my heart. Merry Christmas from Cook Children's Hospital.

A few days before we left for home, I talked to each and every one of the nurses and the therapists who worked so beautifully with Luke. I had one question for them: "Are y'all giving up on my son?" One by one they assured me that Luke would make more progress at home, and that this will be the best thing for Luke. I understood, for the most part.

Cook threw a party for Luke, and the staff brought us gifts. One of the gifts was a picture of Luke and me sleeping in his hospital bed, which still hangs in Luke's room. Those nurses will always be in my heart. And I thank them for taking care of Luke and for keeping me sane.

I had driven every Tuesday and every Friday to see Luke. And each time, there was a lump in my throat as I approached the hospital. But by the end of the four months, the feeling had gone away. Cook had become a place of comfort, love, and support. I will forever be grateful for our time at Cook Children's Hospital and the amazing staff. They saved my life. From here on, it would be exactly as the staff always reminded me: "It's in God's hands."

Tim Siegel, 1/4/16

On Wednesday, Jenny and I will depart Cook Children's hospital with Luke and head home. Our family will be under the same roof for the first time since the morning of July 28. As I stare into Luke's beautiful blue eyes, I think about our two long hospital stays. Chapter 1: July 28–September 10 (UMC) Chapter 2: September 10–January 6 (Cook Children's Hospital). As we begin Chapter 3, Jenny and I are anxious, nervous, and excited. But we are confident more miracles are in store for our little miracle. From cardiac arrest to multiple surgeries, to blood pressure issues to constant vomiting, to finding his voice and following some commands, Luke has fought and fought and fought for the last 160 days. And he is not done. We believe he will thrive at home with family, friends, and therapy. We know he has a very, very long road ahead of him. But the coach in me knows that with hard work, and love and encouragement, anything is possible. If I ever write a book, I would love to title it "It's in God's Hands." That is what I have heard from doctors, nurses, and so many

others—I believe that. Going home will
be hard for me. Seeing his buddies, his
baseball team, and all of the other things
that will trigger the emotions. But we
have family and we will be okay. Cook
Children's has been family, everyone on
staff has been absolutely amazing. We
are forever grateful. And so grateful to
have all of you in our lives. God Bless.

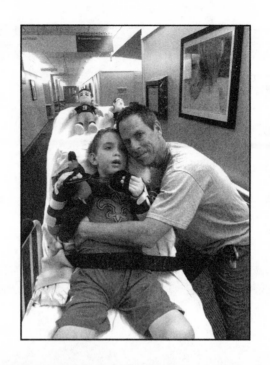

four

MY EARLY YEARS

My parents grew up in Long Island, New York, and settled in Manhasset on the North Shore to start a family. When I was two years old, we moved south to New Orleans for my dad's real estate consulting job. I am the second of my parents' four children. My brother Bobby is five years older than me and is an unbelievably talented classical pianist. My brother Chris is fourteen months younger than me and is a realtor in Newnan, Georgia. He and his wife Monica have two beautiful girls. My sister, Victoria, is five years younger than me and lives in Madison, Wisconsin with her husband and three brilliant children.

Our family is a typical family. We fought. We loved. We haven't always seen eye to eye with each other, but we are blessed with loving, supportive parents, who just celebrated their sixty-third wedding anniversary in 2019.

My mom is quite the worrier, often up at night thinking about others. But she cares for her four children and her nine grandchildren with all her heart and soul. My dad may be the most brilliant man I've ever meet. There's not one topic or subject that he doesn't know about. My parents were there for me during my junior tennis days, as they sent me to tournaments all over the country. They are with me today during these incredibly difficult days. They hurt for their son, and they ache for their grandson.

Tim Siegel, 10/27/18

Tonight, it's just Luke and me at home. We are watching the World Series and a little college football. I always think about the sporting events Luke has missed, because there was nothing he loved more. But tonight, it's not about sports. The seventh and eighth grade Belles and Beaux dance is going on as I write this. I pictured Luke and Ellie going together, and Luke hanging out with all of his buddies. I am also hoping that Jenny is doing ok, as she is a chaperone. I can't imagine what she is going through while watching all of Luke's friends looking great and having a blast. I really do want Luke included in all of that. Not just sporting events. But I am also sensitive to his friends, and I don't want to take away from their joy tonight. The funny thing about tonight is that if Luke were at Belles and Beaux, he would probably want to come home early so that he could watch the World Series with me. Oh God, I don't have the words to express my sadness when there is a sporting event on TV. It's as if I grieve harder, and with more intensity, when I watch sports without feedback from my little buddy. But I know it's good for Luke to hear me talk about the games. And I will never stop! Tomorrow night, I will be by his side when our Saints take on the Vikings. Luke started out slowly in Fort Worth this week. But it was great to be back among all of his loving therapists. We spent quality time today watching Ellie win the city championship in volleyball. So good to be around my girls. Have a wonderful Sunday.

My childhood was tennis, tennis, and more tennis. I started playing at the age of six. I loved it, and I was so passionate about the game. Success came early for me, which only fueled my passion and competitiveness. At twelve years old, I was ranked first in the South, and fourth in the country. Having success at an early age was both good and challenging. It was good because my interest and love of the game continued to rise with each tournament victory. But it was also difficult to live up to expectations. Especially my own.

Tennis is the ultimate individual sport, but I believe it's important to play team sports. Playing team sports teaches you everything that is important in life. Teamwork, playing together and for each other, leadership, and accepting your role. I played flag football, basketball, baseball, and ran track until eighth grade, but tennis was always my number one love.

I practiced almost every day. I certainly had pressure to win, but that pressure came from me and no one else. There was no place I would rather be than on a tennis court. I was so fortunate to have parents who did not pressure me, as they rarely watched me practice. They simply supported me and expected me to work hard. My parents knew I was driven to be the best I could be. When I was young, a reporter asked me what my goals were in tennis, and I responded that I was going to be a professional tennis player. In my mind, that was understood. I played tournaments from age seven to eighteen. I won a few national tournaments, including the National Clay Courts and a couple of national doubles tournaments. I was one of the top doubles players in the country, but I was never satisfied. One year, I also won the Sportsmanship Award at the USTA Nationals in Kalamazoo, an honor that ranks as one my top accomplishments, seeing as my temper was an issue in my early teen years. My goal was to improve daily.

I knew early in my career that for me to compete at the professional level, it was going to be in doubles. I loved doubles. The strategy, my aggressive nature, having a partner, made it a natural fit for me. In the juniors, most players focus on their singles game, but I did the opposite.

I chose to play college tennis at the University of Arkansas. The Razorback tennis program was one of the best in the nation. I was so excited to be playing for a great team, and for a university with so much school spirt and a tradition of winning in all sports. College tennis was amazing. The intensity, the crowds, and playing for a great group of guys and coaches made it my most enjoyable days as a tennis player. All four of my years at Arkansas, we finished in the top ten nationally, reaching the quarter of the NCAA championships twice. We won a conference championship, and my highlight individually was reaching the semifinals of the NCAA championship in doubles in 1986.

I began my professional career in January 1987, and I played through the end of 1989—only three years, but three of the best years of my life. I had extreme highs and crushing losses, all part of life on the pro tour. I was fortunate to compete in all four grand slams: Australian Open, French Open, Wimbledon, and US Open. I have lasting memories from each of them. At the Australian Open, after losing in the third round of doubles, my partner Richard Schmidt and I went to the beach to throw the football. Richard broke his foot while catching one of my Drew Brees-like throws. At Wimbledon, my partner Marc Flur and I battled back from two sets down to win our opening match. The feeling after winning a match at Wimbledon was amazing! The atmosphere at Wimbledon is like no other. The fans are passionate, and the crowds are incredible. At the US Open, I signed up at the last minute to play with Brazilian player, Nelson Aerts. Together our ranking put us as the last team to get into the tournament. As we walked out to the courts for our first-round match, we realized we hadn't even discussed which side of the court we would play on. We both preferred to play the ad court, but Nelson opted to play the deuce court. This was actually the scene on the way to our first-round match! Somehow, we upset the sixteenth-ranked team in the world. In round two, we defeated two legends in the game, Paul McNamee and John Lloyd. In the third round, the round of sixteen, we faced the number one team in the world, Stefan Edberg and Anders Järryd. I was honored to be on the same court, but I was also fearful of getting embarrassed. But Nelson and I played an inspired level, and lost to the eventual champions in three sets. I felt like I belonged after that match. In my three years on tour, I played against some of the greatest to ever play the game. I lost to John and Pat McEnroe, defeated Ivan Lendl, and had a win over Yannick Noah and Paul Annacone.

At the end of my second year on tour, I knew that coaching was something I wanted to pursue. While continuing to play doubles, I also coached players on tour. I worked with former number one doubles player Robert Seguso, former top-fifty player Joey Rive, and travelled briefly with other players as well.

One of the greatest highlights of my tennis career happened in San Diego in 1988 at the U.S. Davis Cup, where I watched the U.S. team—Andre Agassi, John McEnroe, and the doubles team, Ken Flach and Robert Seguso—defeat France in a thrilling match. It was my first experience watching a team play so hard for each other and for their country.

Being on tour was awesome. I thoroughly enjoyed the competition and seeing the world. I was lucky to visit Australia, Asia, Europe, Africa and to be in cities like Sydney, Paris, Florence, Tokyo, Seoul, and even Lagos, Nigeria. I wanted to be a coach, so I made the decision to retire from tennis when I was ranked around one hundredth in the world in doubles. However, I regretted the decision for a few years afterwards, wondering if I had retired too soon.

My first job after retirement was as the director of tennis at the Indianapolis Tennis Center. That was in January of 1990. In the summer of that year, I received a call from tennis legend Dennis Ralston asking if I would join him at SMU (Southern Methodist University) in Dallas. For two years, I coached the SMU women's tennis team and assisted Dennis with the men's team. Then in the fall of 1992, T. Jones, the athletic director at Texas Tech, offered me the head coaching position. From January 1993 to July 2015, I was blessed to coach at a wonderful university and in a special community in Lubbock, Texas. Twenty-three years coaching alongside some amazing coaches and working with tremendous administrators.

Tim Siegel, 4/27/17

I knew by the time I was a freshman at The University of Arkansas that I wanted to coach. After retiring from professional tennis, I coached a few players on the tour. I coached 2 years at SMU before coming to Texas Tech in January of 1993. 23 incredible years at Texas Tech. The last 2 years coaching at Cooper High School and the middle schools have been just what I needed. I love kids. And I have loved coaching tennis, but more importantly, I loved talking to the kids about life. Today I told the students at Cooper that this semester will be my last semester coaching. I will continue to teach the tennis classes at Laura Bush, but my coaching days are over. My life, the rest of my life, will be devoted to the Team Luke Foundation. I will give everything I have every day to help families with children who have suffered a brain injury. I won't be coaching at college or high school, but I am coaching another team now. That team is Team Luke! Every day, I think about how proud I was of Luke when he played sports. He was a coach's dream. Played hard, never complained, and hated to lose. He loved to compete. He loved his teammates, and didn't want to let them down. He loved being on a team. Well, today he is on a team. He is the M.V.P. of TEAM LUKE. Yesterday, I felt like I was coaching Luke in this video. We had to beat 35 times. And did he ever. Did this 50 TIMES!!! When Luke practiced, he would say throw me 10 more, or 20 more ground balls. Just like we did in this video. Thank you Texas Tech. Thank you Cooper. I enjoyed it more than you know. Coaching has been in my blood. My passion. But my family has always been my #1 passion. This will allow me to be at every therapy session. And at therapy . . . I coach.

In my twenty-three years as a coach, I did my best to instill in my players to play hard, be on time, and represent Tech with class and integrity. I was proud of the success that our team achieved. We consistently ranked in the top twenty-five nationally and qualified for twelve NCAA Championships. Two of my doubles teams made it to the finals of the NCAA championship, twice coming close to a national championship. We had tremendous support from the community, as we were always near the top in attendance.

But I wanted to do more than coach. I want to teach. I wanted to get to know my players and teach them the importance of discipline, work ethic, playing for each other, and especially the importance of family. I wanted them to be prepared for life after college. Coaching college tennis was far more than working on strokes and strategy. For me it was teaching and coaching life lessons.

I started as a three-time captain leading the University of Arkansas tennis team, spent over two decades coaching college teams, and now I coach a different team: Team Luke.

five

WELCOME HOME, LUKE

On January 5, 2016, I sat next to Luke most of the night and wondered if we were ready to go home. I consulted with the day nurses, the night nurses, and the doctors. They all assured us that it was time to go, and that this was best for Luke and our family. But was Luke ready to go home? Was I ready?

On the morning of January 6, 2016, there were many hugs, and even more tears. For four months and four days, we had lived on the fourth floor of Cook Children's. We said our goodbyes, but I knew we would see each other again. Our new life was about to begin, and I was anxious, nervous, and unsure. I wasn't confident we would be ok, but Cook Children's taught me a lot, especially about myself. We were going home to a different life, but I knew I was strong enough to handle whatever challenges lay ahead.

We headed towards Lubbock on a cold, cloudy day. Jenny drove, Alex was in the front seat, and I sat in the back next to Luke. It was an uneventful trip, thank goodness. We stopped once to feed Luke through his gastrostomy tube (G-tube), since he couldn't yet eat or drink orally, and to change him. He seemed content.

My stomach began to churn as we got closer to Lubbock. We had agreed to meet some of Luke's supporters in the parking lot of the baseball field, where he used to compete, before going home. A friend had posted on Facebook that we would be arriving in town around 6:00 p.m. Everyone was encouraged to bring a sign welcoming Luke back home. By the time we arrived, the temperature had dropped, and it was bitterly cold and raining.

THE BACKYARD

Luke,

As I write this to you, I am staring at our backyard. OUR backyard. Do you remember when we were building this house, all you ever asked was whether it would be big enough to throw long passes. I answered the same way every time you asked. "Just wait, you'll see." The backyard was always our place. Our time to improve your baseball skills, and our place to get away from the girls. That's what you said. I can picture us at our old house on 104th That is where you learned how to catch pop ups. We didn't have much room thanks to Mom and her landscaping. But we made it work. Boy did we ever. We spent hours and hours working on your arm, scooping up ground balls, and trying to avoid the big tree. You know what I loved more than anything? You NEVER said no when I asked if you wanted to play catch. I used to daydream about having a son who wanted to play catch. And you were that son. You are that son. We had so many special times in that backyard. Occasionally we would shoot hoops, or ride our bikes, and of course we had to go to the front yard to throw the football. Every second together was magical. But that backyard was ours. I taught. You learned. We talked about sports, school, and anything that came to our minds. When you were about seven, you said something I will never forget. "Dad, I wish we had a bigger backyard, but it's ok that we don't." I told your mom it was time for daddy's boy to have more space. We moved into our rent house for almost a year, while our dream backyard was being built. Even though our rent house was small, with a tiny backyard, I was excited and so were you. BECAUSE we moved right next to a park. We had all the space we needed. I loved telling Mom that we would be back soon, we were headed to the park. Every day. There was a moment in our rent house that comes to mind nearly every day. It was sort of a father son bonding moment that sticks with me. I didn't have the key to get in our house. We were stuck outside waiting for Mom and the girls. My phone had died, which as you know happened a lot. You know what you said to me? "No problem dad, our gloves are in the car. Let's just throw the ball until they get home." We threw and we talked, and we threw and we talked. I felt like I was talking to my 15-year-old son, not my 7-year-old. I don't why that memory stands out, because we had millions of memories. Finally our new house was built. There was only dirt in the backyard when we moved in, but you were finally satisfied that OUR backyard was big enough to throw long passes. I told mom no landscaping and no trees in the backyard. We needed space. This was going to be perfect. Just you and me. I guess we could have included the girls, don't you think? I have to tell you something buddy. Every day I take the trash to the dumpster, I think about what could have been, what should have been. I walk through our backyard, and I swear sometimes I see you throwing a perfect strike to me. I also picture throwing a hard one to you, and it sails right over your head into the neighbor's yard. We do rock, paper, scissors to see who gets it. And before I head to the back gate, you are on your way to retrieve my bad throw. You know, it's not just the throwing I miss. It's the talks. I can only imagine what they would have been like. My heart hurts. My stomach hurts. If you saw me now, you would say in your sweet voice, "Dad, why are you crying, it will be ok." I am so sorry buddy. I am so sorry that we never got to throw in OUR backyard. Even though we never had the chance to play catch, there are things that have taken its place. Sitting in your bed with you, driving to Fort Worth, walking around the neighborhood, listening to the girls talk about whatever it is they talk about, watching you in therapy. Telling you about our Saints. I am still your Dad. And you are still my son. And I will do everything I can every single day the rest of my life to help you get better. You are my boy.

Love,
Dad.

Engine 12, the first responders to Luke's accident on that fateful July day, asked to lead us into the parking lot. With their siren blaring, we followed behind them heading toward the ballfield. My stomach was in knots, and my heart was racing. I wasn't sure what to expect. When we turned on Milwaukee Avenue, I couldn't believe my eyes. There were at least 200 people lined up on both sides of the parking lot in the cold and rain. We drove slowly past the cheers, the tears, and all the signs. We looped back around so that people on both sides had the chance to see Luke. It felt like we were in a parade, with the loud cheers of "Hey Luke, we love you!" and "Welcome home, Luke!" It was a beautiful scene, and I remember it fondly every time I drive past the field. As we left the parking lot and turned for home, I looked to the west, and there was a beautiful sunset, just beyond the rain and clouds. Was that a sign from God? I choose to believe so.

We arrived at the house and were greeted with a welcome home sign for Luke in the front yard. We'd had a wheelchair ramp installed outside, and fortunately the inside of the house was already wheelchair accessible. I carried Luke from the car and settled him into the recliner. Luke's loyal eight-year-old cockapoo, Saint, greeted us at the door. Saint hadn't seen Luke since July, and today he saw a very different Luke than he remembered. It didn't matter though, as Saint immediately climbed next to Luke on the recliner and put his face on Luke's leg. He knew, somehow he knew. Since then, anyone who comes to visit Luke must deal with a very protective dog.

The first few weeks at home were a blur. We had visitors nonstop. We tried our best to follow our new routine, which felt more like chaos than structure. Jenny and I had to find a way to incorporate Luke into the lives of the girls and vice-versa. We had a schedule for Luke's medications, which took me a few days to learn. He took meds for seizures and for his stomach. He took Zoloft for his mood. He was still taking Sinemet, which occasionally made him nauseated. Everything carried a great deal of importance, and there was no room for error. I was already feeling stressed. A few days into being home, I was feeling down but did all I could not to show it. I was attempting to administer Luke's meds, but it wasn't going into the tube easily. Jenny suggested that his extension might be clogged. I didn't listen. I forced the medication in, and suddenly it all flew out onto the carpet, making a huge mess. Jenny was upset with me. I was upset with myself, that I'd let my stubbornness and bad attitude affect Luke. I wanted to crawl into a hole. I wanted to scream.

Luke began therapy at Pediatric Therapy Inc. the next week, on January 11. Jenny and I met with the therapists who would be working with Luke—Pam, Katie, and Monica. After discussing their plans for Luke's treatment, we were confident PTI was the right place. Over the course of the year, Luke was going to have physical therapy at PTI, and occupational therapy and speech therapy at home. I insisted on being at every therapy session. I wanted Luke to know I was there. And I wanted to be there to coach Luke, to inspire and motivate him. That first year, and even now, my mood and my attitude are determined by how well Luke does at therapy. Did he respond? Was he alert? Did he finish the session?

Many of his therapy sessions were cut short because he would start dry-heaving and throwing up. We don't know what the exact reason was, but we figured out that any change of movement would initiate it. I don't know how many times I would hold his blue emesis bag while he threw up. His sad eyes looking at me while he got sick. It was one of the hardest things for me to watch. We learned that we had to give his food and medication at least an hour before therapy.

I believed Luke would improve with hard work, love, support, strong faith, and hope. My patience and optimism didn't waver as I watched Luke in therapy every day of the week for an entire year. I had heard stories of children who didn't speak for five years after their accident, and then somehow they began to talk. It could happen for Luke. I could wait.

Speech therapy focused on improving Luke's ability to

eat and to communicate non-verbally. Luke worked quite a lot on swallowing, practicing with small sips of frozen lemonade, water, apple sauce, and ice cream. He was making great progress and soon enjoying his favorite candy, Sour Patch Kids. He would suck on one end as I held up the other, his tongue moving rapidly, excitedly. The speech therapist also worked with Luke on eye-gazing. It helped him use his eyes to communicate. The therapist would hold up two cards with objects he recognized, and he would look for the card with the item called out. We were still unsure how well Luke could see, especially out of his left eye.

In his physical and occupational therapy sessions, he works on head control, rolling, sitting to standing, hand and leg movement, and stretching. Some days, Luke is alert and responsive. Others, not at all. We learned that it is better for Luke to be upright as much as possible, rather than sitting in his chair or laying in his bed all day. Moving his muscles and bones is crucial to his posture. We have a stander at home that Luke is on for at least an hour each day. We also have bolsters to help stretch and work on his spine. As he continues to grow, we adjust his wheelchair to accommodate his height. Unfortunately, Luke's spine is more than 55 percent curved, making scoliosis a big concern. It's likely that he will have yet another surgery to correct it.

We are so grateful for the PTI therapists who have patiently worked with Luke over these last three years, especially Katie who has been with Luke since day one. Each therapist brings a unique perspective, a different personality, and a lot of experience—but each shows the same tremendous love for Luke. They have gotten to know him, and admire how hard he works. They play videos of New Orleans Saints games and Ed Sheeran songs to wake him up and to motivate him. And as has often been discussed, they all love Luke's eyelashes.

Tim Siegel, 8/27/17

I thought I was ready for last night. Meet the Pirates at Cooper High School is a wonderful night of school spirit, as a few thousand Pirate fans were there to celebrate the start of the new year. I dropped off Kate with no intention of staying, but Jenny convinced me to visit for just a few minutes. Despite my reservations, I was appreciative of the many people who came up to Luke and me. The constant hellos and brief encounters were comforting, and didn't give me time to think about what Luke was missing. Until we went on the track. The picture of Luke and his friends was painful. So many thoughts went through my head in a matter of seconds. Then minute by minute I changed. I saw people who heightened my anxiety. I watched as Luke's friends were running around with big smiles

on their faces. Buddies of mine were
visiting, and I had no interest in joining
them. Suddenly, I had such a big pit in
my stomach; I had to leave. And the
worst part is that Kate had not yet been
introduced as a freshman varsity volleyball player. I sat in the car, took a deep
breath, and sadly drove home. I pictured
Luke running around with his friends. I
thought of all of the people I said hello to,
wondering if I had shown my pain. Last
night used to be the kind of night I loved.
Not anymore. Not now. I was so proud
of Kate and Ellie. They looked beautiful
and happy. I loved watching Ellie cheer
with energy and joy. After unloading Luke
into his recliner, I felt so much anxiety
and rage that I needed to walk it off. This
was when I asked Luke if he wanted to
go for a walk. His response made my
night. An hour later, Jenny came home,
and I immediately knew that this night
was just as hard on her. We talked about
the warmth we felt. We also talked about
those who avoided us. I hurt for Jenny.
And I know she worries about me. This
is life. Hard beyond words. Watching
everyone laughing and having fun didn't

seem right. Didn't seem fair. Didn't seem real. But today is a new day. A new opportunity to make a difference with my family. With my foundation. Tomorrow is the start of the new school year. I will be taking Luke to school in the morning. The first day excitement of the students and their parents. And the pit in my stomach as I run into his friends. Please pray for Jenny during this time. And my girls. And for Luke as we prepare for our trip to Fort Worth on Wednesday.

My life today has few similarities to my life before the accident. For as long as I can remember, my plans were dictated by the seasons, mostly whatever sport was in season. Even as a college tennis player and coach, there were three distinct seasons the dictated our lives: spring was dual-match season; summer was camps and recruiting season; fall was individual-tournament season. Today, my life with Luke has no seasonality. Every day is basically the same routine. Therapy every day of the week.

Luke is my son. My only son. My hero. My inspiration. My little athlete. My boy. And I will be in therapy with him every single day that I can. For the rest for my life. Even still, every morning I wake up and pray that today will be different, that something new will happen. Will he set a new personal best for how long he holds his head up, or will he consistently kick the ball with both feet? Maybe he will roll over with absolutely no help. And the big one that I wait for, will he say Dad, Mom, Saints, or Drew Brees? I'm convinced his first words will be one of those. I don't know when it will happen, but I know it will.

I am not a fan of the phrase "new normal," as there is nothing normal about our new life, but this is our routine now. There is an unattributed quote that I've come to love: "When you can't control what's happening, challenge yourself to control the way you respond to what's happening. That is where your power is." This is what I aim to do every day.

six

GOD THINGS

An occurrence or an event that has great impact on someone's life or circumstance is often referred to as "a God thing." Are they signs with a bigger meaning or just simple coincidences? I have asked myself this time and time again over the last few years when a chance meeting or surprise encounter turned out to be an answered prayer, or an unexpected moment felt like God was talking to me. I'm a firm believer that you can find meaning in everything.

Tim Siegel, 5/27/17

> I have been asked so many times in the last 23 months this question: Do you feel guilty for trying to be happy? Is that why

you can't find joy or happiness? That isn't the case. It is simply because my heart hasn't allowed it to happen. Until last night. U2 has been one of my top 2 bands (Springsteen the other) of all time. I first saw them in 1987, and have seen them over 10 times since that memorable night. U2 has a special place in my marriage as well. Jenny and I got engaged in April of 2001, the night we saw U2. Our wedding song was "Beautiful Day." Those words are written inside my ring. Last night I took Jenny, Kate, and Ellie to Cowboys stadium hoping beyond hope that they would like it . . . and that I would let myself go to a place I haven't been in 23 months. A U2 concert is like a religious experience for me. A spiritual 2 hours. It was absolutely amazing. I am a concert guy. I have been to well over 100 concerts, but this one ranks near the top because I didn't expect to feel this. I honestly didn't know that I could. The only thing that could have made it better was to have Alex and Matt with us. But Alex is home taking wonderful care of Luke. The day started with an email saying that my tickets had been upgraded because of an error. Amazing seats. And it ended with every possible hit played in between the full album of *The Joshua Tree*, which I think is one of the greatest albums of all time. I can't wait to get back tonight to hold my boy and tell him how much I love him. But until then . . . I will enjoy every moment with Jenny and the girls.

I love music, especially classic rock. I am a big fan of the Eagles and U2. And my all-time favorite musician is Bruce Springsteen. For thirty-five years, Springsteen's music has resonated with me like no other. When Kate, Ellie, and Luke were much younger, they listened to Bruce every day. They were too young to complain. On a family road trip one summer, we played a game where they would guess Springsteen song titles with one-word clues. The three of them came up with fifty Springsteen songs. It was a proud dad moment.

For me, tennis and music went hand in hand. I associated certain songs with tournaments that I played. As a young kid traveling all over Louisiana, I had listened mostly to the Beatles and ELO (Electric Light Orchestra). The week leading up to my National Doubles 18 and Under win, I had blasted the *Eagles Greatest Hits* on my walkman. When I traveled Europe early in my professional career, U2's *The Joshua Tree* album was my companion on train and plane rides.

Music is something else Luke and I share. Luke loves listening to Ed Sheeran, and we play his music for Luke every day. Luke and I were lucky enough to meet Sheeran backstage at a Dallas concert in August of 2017. I told him that his music helps Luke, and that he moves his tongue in response when I ask him if he wants to hear Ed Sheeran. Sheeran was very kind and even wore his Team Luke bracelet during the concert!

Music had always been a part of my life, but that changed on July 28, 2015. After Luke's accident, I had no desire to listen to music. I didn't want to hear songs that were uplifting, and certainly didn't want to listen to sad songs. The two times I drove home from the hospital to get clothes, I kept the radio off. My standoff with music lasted nearly three weeks.

On day nineteen, I drove home to check on Saint and felt this urge to turn on the radio. I resisted. But as I pulled out of the driveway to head back to the hospital, I stopped the car. I felt a strong need to turn on the satellite radio to channel twenty, which of course was Bruce Springsteen's channel. Something told me to turn on the radio, or was it *someone*. I sat in the driveway for a minute before I turned on the radio, and when I did one of Bruce Springsteen's least popular songs came on, "Countin' on a Miracle." I bet I have heard that song only two or three times in ten years. And there it was, today of all days. Hearing those words gave me hope. I looked up in the sky and nodded. Was that a sign, a coincidence, or maybe a God thing?

A year later, one day in the middle of August, I was

driving aimlessly around town, feeling sad, depressed, angry. My emotions engulfed me as I drove and drove and drove. I stopped at the Market Street grocery at Quaker and 98th Street. Why there? I don't know. I tended to avoid that store because it is less than a mile from the scene of Luke's accident. Whenever I drove down Quaker, there was a pit in my stomach. I literally turned my head in the opposite direction to avoid seeing it. I vaguely remember where I parked that afternoon. I sat in my car in complete silence, my head was down. There was a knock on my window, which startled me. A man looked inside and said, "Hey, I'm praying for you. One foot in front of the other." Then he walked away.

One foot in front of the other. People often approach me to express their love and support for Luke. We've gotten used to it. But this was different. Now, I was down, lower than I had ever felt, and a stranger approached me with a simple but profound statement: one foot in front of the other. I sat in the car thinking about those words, and three thoughts popped in my mind.

1. We all take for granted our ability to put one foot in front of the other.
2. There are days I can barely get out of bed, therefore struggling to put one foot in front of the other.
3. We hope and pray that one day Luke will be able to put one foot in front of the other.

My daughter Kate has played basketball since she was in third grade. She loves the game. Prior to her freshman year of high school, she and her varsity teammates played in a few team camps. One such camp was held in the middle of June 2017, at the University of Texas at Arlington. Jenny and I took Luke to watch his sister do what she loves to do. The team had won their first game, and, as Luke and I waited for the second game, a woman approached us. Usually when this happens, I get a sympathetic nod. Every so often I'll receive a pleasant hello. There have been times when people have stopped me to pray for us at that moment. This time, the woman walked right past us, head down, without lifting her eyes. She did not acknowledge us. About five feet beyond our seats, she turned and said, "You were chosen for this." And walked away. I was too stunned to respond.

Every so often we would experience that kind of random moment. We never quite knew what to make of them. One day, a woman jogging on our block passed our house and waved when she saw us with Luke in the front yard. Next thing we knew, she had turned back and asked to pray for us. She'd had no idea Luke lived on that block. Another day, I was at Market Street grocery with Luke when a woman walked up to us in tears. She said she had prayed to God to meet Luke.

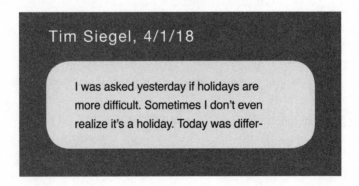

Tim Siegel, 4/1/18

> I was asked yesterday if holidays are more difficult. Sometimes I don't even realize it's a holiday. Today was differ-

ent. Jenny, Kate, Ellie, Luke, and I went to Experience Life this morning. I must admit I was not much in the mood to get out of the house. The Easter service was all about miracles. We were asked to pray for a miracle. I wanted everyone at the service to pray for Luke. I certainly understand that we are not the only family who needs a miracle. But at that time, I felt like the message was directed to us. We are not finished. That was part of the message as well. God knows Luke is not finished. As the service ended, someone on staff asked me if we would like to go in the prayer room and have them pray for us. Very emotional. Very moving. Much appreciated. On our way out, so many people told us that they were praying for us. We heard, "hey Luke" From people we have never met. Every time Luke is prayed for, his eyes are wide open. Every time I tell him that God is right here with him every day, his eyes are wide open. A few minutes ago, I took Luke on our daily walk around the neighborhood. Near the end of our walk, a young boy sees us and yells out, "is that Luke Siegel?" I asked him how he knew Luke, and he told me that he saw him on the news. I took a picture with him. It moved me to see a boy so happy to have met Luke. I pray that all of the families who are suffering, who need a miracle, found peace on this Easter Sunday. And know that God is not finished.

I hate to admit this, but our family has been to church only a couple of times since the accident. It was a special Sunday when all of us, including Luke, could attend Experience Life together. On one rare Sunday, as I sat in the congregation listening to the band, something came over me. I pulled out my phone and, with Jenny glaring at me, sent a text to Pastor Chris asking him to have Brandon Gwinn, the band leader, call me.

The band played a song that sounded like a mixture of U2 and Coldplay, and I wondered if Brandon would write a song for Luke and me, about Luke and me, something that captured us as father and son. I met with Brandon the following week to ask him, and he agreed. A few months later he sent me a text message that the song was finished, with a link to listen. I was amazed. "My Boy (Luke's Song)" may be the most special thing ever given to me. Brandon also made a video to accompany the song. Check it out on YouTube. Thank you, Brandon. And thank God we all went to church that day. Was that a God thing? Absolutely.

Jeff Sparr played tennis for Ohio State during my days at Arkansas. He was now living in Providence, Rhode Island with his family. We hadn't spoken since college. In the winter of 2017, he called to tell me that his son Grayson was a baseball player just like Luke. Grayson wore #2 and Luke wore #3. Jeff and Grayson decided together to raise money for Team Luke by Grayson swinging his bat 100 times a day for 100 days. Imagine swinging the bat 100 times for 100 days in Rhode Island during winter. Every day, Grayson posted a video of his last few swings. Some were inside, some were outside in the snow, and many were in the backyard with his brother or dad pitching the soft toss. His motto was #2 for #3. He asked people to pledge twenty-three dollars.

The local newspaper in Providence ran a story on what Grayson Sparr was doing for a boy he had never met. I was so moved by Grayson's incredible thoughtfulness. I flew out to Providence and pitched him the last 100 swings. *NBC Nightly News* was there to film it. The story caught the attention of America. It was an extraordinary act of kindness, discipline, and support for a boy, and a cause. Jeff and Grayson came to Lubbock several months later for an event we hosted and got to meet Luke. Grayson taught so many kids, and adults, about love, about giving back, and so much more. It was absolutely a God thing.

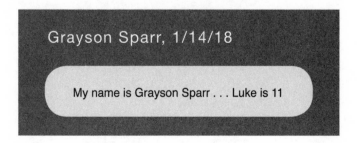

Grayson Sparr, 1/14/18

My name is Grayson Sparr . . . Luke is 11

years old and loves baseball as much as I do. Luke suffered an anoxic brain injury on July 28, 2015. Now he fights every day to get stronger and stronger. To help support Luke in his fight, I am going to practice to get stronger and stronger with him.

seven

FIVE INSPIRATIONS
FROM LUKE

I have always been comfortable with public speaking. As a young child, it was natural for me to speak to a reporter about tennis or to get up and speak in front of my class-mates. In college at the University of Arkansas, I majored in broadcast journalism because I wanted to have my own TV or radio show one day. Talking sports of course. I worked at the local public radio station, KUAF, reading the sports from the associated press (that's what we did back in the early 1980s), and I added to the show by giving my weekly college and pro predictions.

During my coaching years at Texas Tech, the local media were well aware of my passion for sports. For all sports, but especially my Saints. I always had strong opinions and enjoyed sharing them on air. Soon after the Saints won the Super Bowl in Miami in 2010, I started hosting a segment called "Tuesdays with Tim" every Tuesday morning on Double T 104.3 in Lubbock (now Double T 97.3).

A couple of years later, the station offered me my very

own one-hour show called "Coach Speak." Every Monday at 6:00 p.m., we had Texas Tech coaches join me to talk about their teams. We got into great debates about college and pro sports. I loved it. It was my favorite hour of the week. Maybe one day I will try it again. I still follow sports religiously, but it doesn't feel the same since Luke's accident.

At Texas Tech, it was not uncommon for me to speak in front of large groups, promoting Texas Tech athletics and our tennis team. We spoke to potential donors, to FCA organizations, and once a year in front of every Texas Tech athletic employee. It was easy to speak about something I believed in and was passionate about. But that all changed after Luke's accident. I wasn't interested in talking anymore. I was terribly sad and devastated, and probably nervous about breaking down. I declined invitations to speak to schools and college teams.

I made an exception in May of 2016, when Brett Masi, the new tennis coach at Texas Tech, asked me to speak to the team before their first-round match at the NCAA Championships. I felt a pit in my stomach as I drove to the McLeod Tennis Center. It was the first time I had been on campus since the accident. Texas Tech was life before the accident. Twenty-three wonderful years as the tennis coach of Texas Tech, and I had avoided the campus for ten months. I was the guy who wouldn't miss any Tech athletic event, and now couldn't even drive on the campus.

But on that day in May, I decided it was time. As I walked up with Luke, I felt like a stranger. Those were my courts. That was my team. I thought about the special times our family had watching my team. I pictured

Luke with me at practice. I remember when he brought his buddy Will to practice. They threw the ball while I worked with my team. Luke loved being with the guys. They loved him. The last time Luke was at our courts had been a very special moment. We had just beaten a good team from the Big 12, and I invited Luke into the locker room to listen to me talk to the team. As I finished, I gathered everyone together, including Luke, we put our hands together, and after the one-two-three count everyone yelled Luke's name. His smile was wide, his hat almost covered his embarrassed eyes.

That last time, in April 2015, Luke had walked into the locker room. Now, I wheeled Luke in, my stomach in knots. The room was silent. I recounted my memory of our last visit, and that was all I could get out before breaking down. I told the team good luck and left with tears streaming down my face. As I sat in the car trying to gather myself, I looked out and felt sick to my stomach. UMC was directly across the street. I felt paralyzed. I couldn't move for what seemed like an hour. Memories of those forty-four days in that hospital hit me like a tidal wave.

In August, I received a phone call from Coach Sylas Politte, the head of the Fellowship of Christian Athletes (FCA). He asked if I would be interested in speaking at the first FCA meeting at Laura Bush Middle School, where my girls attended. This talk, on August 25, was my official return to public speaking. Since then, I have spoken to thousands of kids in elementary and high school, to college teams, youth groups, businesses, men's groups, and at graduations. I have shared our story, my message of hope, throughout Texas and Arkansas. I have thoroughly enjoyed talking to everyone, but especially to middle-school students. They listen intently. Their eyes wide open.

That night before my first talk at my daughters' school, I sat in bed next to Luke, thinking about what I wanted to say. I wanted my message to resonate with everyone. I spent a few hours wondering how I could impact these students. I didn't want this to be only about Luke.

Luke,

When I wake up . . .
When I sneeze . . .
When I watch sports . . .
When I see a baseball field . . .
When I see one of your friends . . .
When I see one of his parents . . .
When I hear a song you liked . . .
When I hear a song that reminds me of you . . .
When I ask a friend how their kids are doing . . .
When I drive to Texas Tech . . .
When I go to sporting events at Texas Tech . . .
When I see a little boy ride his bike . . .
When it's football season . . .
When it's basketball season . . .
When it's baseball season . . .
When I watch your sister play basketball . . .
When I eat with your mom and sisters . . .
When it's a holiday . . .
When I see your nephew . . .
When I drive by a school . . .

When I see a father and son together . . .
When I see a family eating at a restaurant . . .
When I drive by a park . . .
When your friends are on vacation . . .
When it's time to go back to school . . .
When I see a father and son talking . . .
When I see a father and son playing catch . . .
When your friends have a game . . .
When I am driving . . .
When the Saints are playing . . .
When any team is playing . . .
When I see people selling newspapers on the
street . . .
When I drive by our old neighborhood . . .
When I think about middle school sports . . .
When I see a little boy doing something nice for
someone . . .
When someone asks how I am doing . . .
When I ask a friend how their kids are doing . . .
When I see someone wearing Under Armour . . .
When I see someone wearing Texas Tech . . .
When I see kids swimming . . .
When I look at my bracelet . . .
When I look at my necklace . . .
When I see the # 3 . . .
When I see an ambulance . . .
When I see a fire truck . . .
When I see a golf cart . . .
When I see someone in a wheel chair . . .
When Mom and I are alone . . .
When I go to bed . . .

When I pray . . . .

I THINK ABOUT YOU.

I came up with five key points I wanted to make.

FIND YOUR PASSION.

I lost my passion after Luke's accident. Before, the word that best described me would have been "passionate." Passionate about sports. Passionate about the Saints. Passionate about the great university I worked for. Passionate about the Arkansas Razorbacks, my alma mater. Passionate about coaching. And most of all, passionate about my family. I have a wonderfully talented, hard-working, beautiful wife. She is the rock of our family. There is absolutely nothing I enjoy more than spending time with my children. At home, at a game, in the car, watching TV. I love being a dad. I was always a very passionate, positive, upbeat person. As a child, as a teenager, as a collegiate tennis player, and as a husband and father. There were rare times when I would be down, like when my tennis team lost a heartbreaker, or that certain team from New Orleans lost on a last second play (the Minnesota Miracle still gets me down, and of course the heartbreaking loss to the Rams), but the passion never left. My passion is slowly, but surely coming back. My passion now is to help others. My message to students is that they need to find something they are passionate about, and to not let anyone or anything get in their way.

DON'T EVER QUIT.

When I coached at Texas Tech, I loved watching my players give everything they had. I demanded it. I expected toughness from them every time they stepped on the court. Play hard or don't play for me. I hated excuses. They battled. I rarely saw my players give in. But I admit, I have had moments when I wondered if I had it in me to keep going. Those long nights waiting for Luke to fall asleep, and then waking up three hours later to turn him. Most of the time it was impossible to fall asleep again. I did not have a full night of uninterrupted sleep in the first two years following Luke's accident. Not once. It might sound like an exaggeration, but it's not.

Most mornings, I struggled to get out of bed. But all I had to do was look to my right and see my little fighter, my little hero, and I found the strength.

My message to students is that there is never a good reason to quit. In school, in sports, in life. Luke played hard. He never gave up. And that has not changed. He inspires me to fight every day. I encourage students to get out their phone and watch a video of Luke on Instagram or Facebook when they feel like quitting. Maybe that ten-second video will change their outlook for the day.

LEAN ON FRIENDS, FAMILY, COUNSELORS, TEACHERS, AND COACHES.

This is a big one. I withdrew from everyone. I couldn't or wouldn't be around anyone. I didn't answer my phone or the doorbell, and I made sure I didn't see anyone when I was out. And yet today, I desperately need my friends and family. Their support is crucial to my healing. I know that my close friends wonder which Tim they are going to see. They think "Should I talk to him?" or "Does he want to be alone?" or "He was doing ok yesterday, but today not so much." This makes it tough, I understand. But my only explanation is that I don't know how I am going to feel from minute to minute. Some things, or people, or places trigger my moods. But the bottom line is that I need my friends. I need the support.

Keeping things inside isn't healthy. We are all guilty of this, and yet I would imagine that most people feel a whole lot better when they share their struggles and their issues with a trusted friend or counselor. Depression, anxiety, fear, and devastation are things that need to be addressed with a professional or with family.

In my short time as a middle school and high school coach, I walked the halls before and after practice. Students who walked alone or walked with their head down always caught my attention. Life is difficult for teenagers. *Were they ok? Has anyone noticed they are sad or depressed? Do they keep things inside?* I have encouraged students to reach out to others. A simple "hello" or eye contact can change someone's frame of mind. Instead of saying, "Let me know if you ever need anything," surprise a friend in need with a simple text saying, "thinking about you." It meant so much to me. Everyone has the ability to make an impact on someone else.

MAKE GOOD CHOICES, BE CAREFUL.
I think our girls have heard me say "make good choices" a time or two, and now I direct it towards the students. Be careful, in all things, but particularly when it comes to safe-

ty. These days it is quite common to see kids under the age of sixteen driving a golf cart on the street unsupervised. In Lubbock, modified golf carts are everywhere. They are taller, faster, heavier, and are more prone to tipping over, which is what happened to Luke. Kids don't think about what could happen to them, so it's up to the parents. I wish parents wouldn't allow young children to operate those dangerous vehicles on the street, especially without a helmet. Currently, there is no law requiring use of seat belts and helmets. There are no regulations for children operating these vehicles on the streets. *Good Morning America* ran a story in August of 2018 about the dangers of golf carts. Kids used to walk or ride bikes around town. Today, kids drive golf carts. But this isn't only about golf carts. It's about being safe. Kids think they are invincible. They don't think that horrible accidents could happen to them. Luke didn't. But it did.

My message to students is to be careful, to make good choices. Because in one split second, your life can change.

HAVE FAITH.
I have no idea how people get through really tough times without faith. Pain lives inside me every day. It sits inside my stomach, and on bad days it moves into my throat. And every single day, my faith is tested. I can only get through the bad days because of my faith. Without it, I wouldn't be able to speak to groups, be the executive director of a nonprofit, or get out of bed some mornings. I have heard people say at least a hundred times, "Everything happens for a reason," but I'm not sure I believe it. What I am certain of is that God gives me the strength

to move forward, make a difference, and have impact. To take what happened and use it to make a difference for others. I feel elated when I speak to people. When someone approaches me after my talk and expresses their love for Luke or how much they pray for us, it is humbling, and I never get tired of hearing it.

A young girl came up to me at a grocery store and said that my talk saved her life. Another girl at a restaurant told me that my message inspired her to make changes in her life. Young students from a school in Austin came up afterwards telling me that they were now going to be on Team Luke. I especially love it when they mention that from now on they will be a fan of the Saints because of Luke. College players have told me that Luke inspired them to work harder and to never take anything for granted. These stories are powerful. God has given me a platform, a mission, a purpose to share our story, our message. I have regained my passion, and I will never quit. I will continue to lean on friends, family, and therapists. My choices will define me. And most of all, my faith will keep me going. For me, for my wife and girls. For my grandson. And for Luke.

My message to the students is to have faith that the hard days and tough times will pass. And when your faith is weak, remember your purpose and that someone somewhere can learn from your experience.

eight

TEAM LUKE
FOUNDATION

I was sitting in the van outside of PTI while Luke had therapy. Normally, I was right by his side doing therapy, but today I came back outside to catch my breath. Feeling overwhelmed and depressed, I turned on the radio. It was dark and gloomy outside. And it was dark and gloomy in the van. It was one of those days.

Just then, my cell phone rang. It was my friend Amy Etchison. She knew that I was sinking fast and wanted to suggest that I consider starting a foundation. Maybe it could give me my life back, she said. My initial reaction was that I had no energy to live, much less start a foundation. How could I find the strength for this when I barely had enough to take care of Jenny, the girls, and Luke. I went home and thought about it later that night. And thought about it some more. A few days went by. Then something hit me. The word "impact" kept rolling around my mind. Again. It had happened before. I called Amy and asked her to meet me in person to discuss it.

Tim Siegel, 7/14/16

I retired from Texas Tech a few years ago because I wanted to make an impact inside the department for our incredible university, and because I wanted to be around my children all the time. But I came back to coach two more years. Last July, I retired from the university I love so much so that I could make an impact on students in middle school and high school in the Cooper School District. And I wanted to attend every practice and game that my kids played. I have heard the word IMPACT a lot lately. People have come up to me daily telling me how much Luke has impacted the way they parent, or the time they now spend with their children, and how they don't take things for granted. I have been told that Luke's determination and fight have impacted adults and children. And many young kids tell me they pray every day for Luke. Some have mentioned that Jenny and I have impacted and inspired them. But I want everyone to know that I have been impacted by all of you. Your love and support are fuel for me to keep going. I need visitors, text messages, phone calls, and those that say they pray for Luke. Now more than ever. Last week I had someone stop me in my car and tell me to put one foot in front of the other. Tonight on my walk, two neighbors said they pray for Luke every day. As I lay here in my bed so incredibly exhausted, I find it difficult to sleep. But my ok days are slightly better than they used to be. Unfortunately, my bad days are worse than ever. Not sure why. But what I do know is that when I have friends drive in from all over Texas and Arkansas to visit, I feel blessed. And when I get a text from Kliff Kingsbury asking me to bring Luke to practice, I feel blessed. When Astrid comes to take care of Luke three nights a week, I feel blessed. Thank you all for your continued prayers. Please pray for Luke to continue to improve. I want so desperately to communicate with him. I also pray that I will continue to put one foot in front of the other.

I loved coaching the Texas Tech team and the impact I had on the lives of ten players each year, but there was always something missing. I needed more. Yes, I was doing much more than coaching forehands, backhands, serves, and volleys. I was trying to coach life. Instilling a work ethic, teaching discipline, teamwork, leadership, and much more. But it wasn't fulfilling enough. That's what led me to approach Kirby Hocutt, the Texas Tech Athletic Director, about stepping down as coach. My original idea was to begin a new career in fundraising and marketing for the athletic department. I thought that I would be able to have of an impact on people, travel less, and be with my kids more. We discussed it a few times, but I decided to continue coaching.

A couple of years later, in the spring of 2015, I began to have those feelings again. The word "impact" kept coming back to me. How could I impact more people, stay at home more, and still love what I was doing? This time, however, I thought about coaching middle school and high school, and teaching on the side. Yes, I would be giving up a great job. But for me, more success didn't translate into more enjoyment. There was always pressure to win, mostly self-inflicted, that kept me up at night.

Tim Siegel, 7/14/16

Today was a special day. But a very, very tough one as well. Luke had 36 of his closest friends at the house for his 10th birthday (actual bday is tomorrow). So great to have everyone at the house . . . But to look in the backyard and see everyone running around while Luke was vocal in his wheelchair. It was all I could do to not get emotional and sad. Thank you Head Football Coach Kliff Kingsbury for being here. And for the balloons and cookies! An amazing coach and person. Thank you all for being here with us today. And every day. We need you all for your support and prayers. Luke got video messages from Elvis Andrus of the Texas Rangers, David Thomas of the Long-horns and my New Orleans Saints, Jace Amaro of the Red Raiders and the Jets, Toddrick Gotcher of Red Raider basketball. So special. I will share these in the coming days.

I met with Keith Bryant, the Lubbock Cooper school superintendent, a few times in the spring of 2015 to talk about the possibility of me coaching in the school district. That would be the ideal situation for me because I could coach at the same two schools my kids would be attending. I figured I could coach until Luke graduated from high school. Nine more years. The talent level obviously would not be the same. The salary not even close. But none of that mattered. Being around kids every day, getting them excited about playing tennis, teaching them how to compete, and most of all having a bigger impact on their lives during those critical years, that is what appealed to me. When a position opened, I resigned from Texas Tech. That was on July 8, 2015. Luke's accident happened just twenty days later.

The two years I spent coaching at Laura Bush Middle School and Cooper High School are a blur. I was there physically, but emotionally I was with Luke. I did the best I could. I tried to impact those kids with everything I had. But looking back, they had more impact on my life than I did on theirs. They helped me get out of bed. They kept me alive. They made me smile. But ultimately, it was impossible to think that I could give them what they deserved.

I thought about all of this during my meeting with Amy to discuss the possibility of starting a foundation. I didn't know the first thing about foundations, but I was more than ready to learn. I loved the idea of impacting lives while taking care of Luke. Helping other families would be the one way I could begin to live again. This was my opportunity to make something good out of something so bad.

On Labor Day in 2016, Amy and I met with Kade Wilcox, the CEO of Primitive Social, to talk about creating a website and to draft a mission statement. We spent a few hours trying to find the right wording and the right amount of words. We eventually decided that our mission was: *To bring awareness and provide critical support and assistance to families with children who have suffered an anoxic or traumatic brain injury.*

Then I started making phone calls. I called people who ran foundations. I called people in Lubbock who might want to be on my board. I spent the next four months gathering information, putting together my board, creating a website, designing a logo, and choosing the name for the foundation. Jenny and I came up with designs for shirts, sweatshirts, hats, and bracelets. The marketing person in me wanted to see our brand all over Lubbock, the state of Texas, and ultimately the country.

The Team Luk3 Foundation officially launched on January 17, 2017. I was aware that having Luke's name in the foundation name could cause some confusion, since none of the money was going to Luke or to our family. But I decided that Luke's name had to be included. We changed the "E" to a "3" to represent his jersey number, and because the number three was my favorite number growing up playing tennis. Also, Jenny was a very good high-school basketball player in nearby Lorenzo, and her jersey number was three. Luke's favorite number was also three.

I needed a game plan, a strategy, and an awful lot of help. Between January and June of 2017, we had four board meetings. I was blessed and honored to have fifteen wonderful people on the board. It was critical for me to have a well-rounded board of men and women who all had the same goals, who wanted to make a difference in the lives of families going through the unthinkable.

Fundraising was an essential part of Team Luke growing into a successful nonprofit. We needed a good staff, brochures, and other materials. We needed to meet with hospitals and social workers and to present care packages and resource guides to families.

There were challenges those first six months. I began

to feel overwhelmed trying to juggle my work on the foundation, taking Luke to therapy and caring for him, and giving my wife and the girls the love and attention they so desperately needed.

TEAM LUKE HOPE FOR MINDS

Countless friends and strangers reached out to us on Facebook, usually through Jenny. They offered support and prayers. She shared these with me, but I barely remember hearing any of the stories. I don't know if I blocked it out because I simply wasn't ready to hear it.

Tim Siegel, 9/4/17

Luke's wonderful 3rd grade teacher came to see Luke yesterday. Luke absolutely loved Mrs. Julian. She had made Luke this scrapbook and wanted me to add a letter Luke had written to her. Luke had written the letter apologizing for his behavior, despite doing nothing wrong.

He didn't want his friends to miss recess. So, he took the blame. Mrs. Julian mentioned that this happened multiple times, especially when it meant missing recess. He didn't want to miss playing football at recess. She also said that Luke always made sure to include everyone in the game. It was so good to see Mrs. Julian and her daughter, Alyssa. But it really hit me shortly after she left. Those stories brought a smile to my face, but also put me in a funk. It felt good to hear these stories for the first time, but it ripped my heart out that we don't get to see that anymore. We see his fighting spirit. We see his love for his family and friends. But we don't see his amazingly big heart. And his sweet disposition. One day … 18-time grand slam winner Chris Evert sent Luke this message. She and Brad Gilbert were on the air for their US Open set when I texted Brad to see if Chris would send a video. They went to a commercial break and 30 seconds later, I received this beautiful video. Amazing! I hope everyone has a safe and happy Labor Day.

In early 2017, a woman named Ronda Johnson reached out to Jenny on Facebook. Ronda tried multiple times to offer us help through her nonprofit, Hope4Minds, that provided support to children with brain injury. At the time, I hadn't been open to receiving help.

In June of 2017, Jenny mentioned that Ronda Johnson had reached out again to offer financial support. This time, though, I was interested in talking to her. Not for money, but because she was the director of a nonprofit, and I wanted to pick her brain. I contacted her and two days later drove to Austin to meet up with her.

She had started Hope4Minds six years before, after a friend's son's near-fatal drowning. I was impressed with the amount of work she had done through her nonprofit, all by herself. She raised money, put on events, met with families, reached out for sponsors, took care packages to hospitals, met with social workers, and on and on and on. I have no idea how she did all of that. There were two areas she said she needed help. She was uncomfortable getting in front of people to speak, and her least favorite thing to do was fundraising. I smiled at her and said that those were my strengths. I looked at Ronda and said, "Why don't we consider merging our nonprofits?"

After our three-hour meeting, I went back to Lubbock and called an emergency board meeting. Although Team Luke had only been in existence for six months, I approached my board with the idea of a possible merger. A few weeks later, Ronda flew to Lubbock to meet the team. She impressed everyone with her work ethic, her attention to detail, and most of all her energy and passion. For the next six months, we worked out the details to complete the merger. We had a tremendous amount of work to do: loads of paperwork, creating a new website, and assembling our new board. And of course, we needed a new name. Team Luke Hope for Minds was launched in January of 2018.

We came up with a new mission statement: *To enrich the lives of children with a brain injury and give hope to their families through support and education.* We worked with a consultant, set up a budget, defined our short- and long-term goals, formulated a strategic plan, planned events for 2018 and beyond, and hired new employees—an assistant, a social media manager, an intern, and another consultant.

Our first events in 2018 were successful. In February, we had a big team supporting Team Luke Hope for Minds at the Austin Marathon. March is Brain Injury Awareness Month, and several restaurants in Lubbock donated a portion of the proceeds one day to support the foundation. In April, we hosted 180 participants at the Team Luke Hope for Minds Golf Tournament in Austin. In May, we had over 300 runners and walkers at the Team Luke Hope for Minds 5K Fun Run. And, certainly the most exciting for me, Drew Brees headlined the Dinner with Drew, attended by 1,400 of our closest friends, on May 9 in Lubbock. We were on a roll.

Tim Siegel, 3/25/18

I received an email a few weeks ago from Bob Salomon. He heard about Luke's story from a friend. He told me had had written a book called *Beyond the Laces*, and wanted to send us a copy. I feel like this book was written for us. It's about a boy who is sick and loves football. The boy's dad sends a letter to his favorite player, #87. The player sends the boy tickets to the game, and after the big victory, #87 gives the boy the game ball. Sound familiar? #9 gave Luke a game ball!!! This book's message is about inspiring children through kindness. Exactly what Drew Brees has done for Luke, AND what he will be doing for LUKE and Team Luke Hope for Minds ON MAY 9th. Drew Brees is coming to Lubbock for Luke. Still hard to believe. This also reminds me of 2 teams that have shown so much kindness. Friday night, the San Antonio Spurs were so amazing to Luke. The team is full of class. We met them last year, and Friday was just the same. Patty Mills even got a smile out of Luke. And of course, the Texas Tech men's basketball team. Chris Beard, the staff, and every player have allowed Luke in their locker room, their bench, their practices, and their film sessions. Norense Odiase prayed for Luke in the locker room, in Dallas at the NCAA Tournament and at practice. Every player wore Team Luke Hope for Minds shirts on ESPN Gameday. The Team always talks to Luke, and tells me how he inspires them. Chris Beard is a great coach and a great person, and has instilled values and life lessons, which is far more important than X's and O's. Acts of kindness. They go a long way. Especially to little boys who love sports with all their heart. And to little boys who look up to athletes. AND to little boys who are sick or injured. I know that Luke listened to me as I told him about today's game. I also know he will hear me every day, 100 times a day, talk about Drew Brees coming to Lubbock on May 9. I can also guarantee I will see Luke's beautiful smile when I do.

September was our busiest month. We hosted the Pediatric Brain Injury Conference and Resource Fair, a wonderful event for families. The Team Luke Hope for Minds Tennis Classic, a pro women's tennis event, which was held at Texas Tech. And the annual Team Luke Hope for Minds – Play for Luke benefit was in Fort Smith, Arkansas, with Andre Agassi as the headliner.

We made some changes to our profile as well. Hope-4Minds had only supported Texas children eighteen and under who had suffered a brain injury from an accident. With the merger, we expanded our reach to children all over the country. In fact, we helped children in thirteen states in 2018. And we now help children who have suffered a stroke or had an aneurysm. We are so proud that we can offer financial and educational assistance for therapy, ADA home modifications, adaptive toys, durable medical equipment, auto adaptive services, medical claim advocacy, special education advocacy, family counseling, and family getaways. Team Luke Hope for Minds also offers counseling to families and hosts monthly support groups in Austin and in Fort Worth.

Families from all over the country have reached out to us on Facebook, Twitter, and Instagram. We use our social media to connect with them and educate others about brain injuries, treatment, and safety. Every Tuesday is "Tuesday with Tim," where I talk about my experience. On Family Friday, parents share their child's story and how Team Luke Hope for Minds has helped them. On Safety Saturday, we share information to help keep families safe.

In 2018, we gave over $200,000 to families in need and raised over $800,000. Ronda and I are very proud of that. (Parents needing assistance are encouraged to fill out an application on our website, TeamLukeHopeforMinds.org.) The most rewarding part of my job is offering hope and encouragement to parents whose child suffered a brain injury. The stories I hear are powerful, gut-wrenching, and emotional. But it gives me such joy when I hear optimism and hope in their voices. Some parents were given the same grim prognosis, that their child would never do anything. My message to them is that doctors simply don't know what the brain can do after injury. And no MRI can measure the determination and fight of the patient or the amount of love and support a child has, which I believe makes a tremendous difference.

Team Luke Hope for Minds is committed to raising money to help families all over the country. We want to spread awareness about brain injuries. Ronda and I want to be a resource for families and help them see that an anoxic injury or traumatic injury does not mean life is over for the child or the family. Every day, we learn new information about the brain, about new therapies and treatments, and about improvements that happen. It has happened for us, and it can happen for others.

Team Luke Hope for Minds is my new life, my calling, my passion.

ten

NRC: A PLACE OF HOPE

In June of 2016, a friend suggested that I check out the Neurological Recovery Center. He thought the facility might be able to help Luke. I drove to Fort Worth to meet with the owner, Bruce Conti. His passion and his vision are impressive. Bruce and Lee Anne Conti's son Spencer suffered a traumatic brain injury in 2013, during Thanksgiving break of his freshman year of college. Bruce, a real estate developer in Fort Worth, was determined to find the best equipment and the best therapy available for Spencer. When he discovered that companies can't sell therapy equipment to individuals, Bruce opened his own clinic.

Bruce and Lee Anne assumed they would have only a few patients visit their clinic. Today NRC has more than 100 patients. Men, women, and children come from all over the Fort Worth area and beyond to receive treatment. NRC offers physical therapy, aquatic therapy, yoga, and even virtual reality to aid in treatment. The 140,000-square-foot facility houses a variety of therapeutic equipment, including ten Lokomats—a half-a-million-dollar robotic assisted-walking treadmill machine, and the main reason we were considering driving back to Forth Worth every week. The Lokomat is used for highly intensive physiological gait rehabilitation for severely impaired neurological patients and helps with neuroplasticity and recovery in patients with spinal cord injury, stroke, multiple sclerosis, and Parkinson's.

Tim Siegel, 11/9/17

You walk in to the Neurological Recovery Center, and you feel a positive vibe. There is energy and optimism, and hope and encouragement. And plenty of smiles. Everyone feels it. Bruce Conti, whose son suffered an anoxic brain injury, has built the one stop shop for all spinal cord injuries, brain injuries, and strokes. The NRC has everything. But the staff is what makes the NRC a place where you almost forget your pain and suffering. Everyone is in a good mood. The therapists love what they do, and because of that, the patients get better. Mentally and physically. Luke comes to the clinic, and we hear "Hi Luke," and "hey it's Uncle Luke." And even "Go

Saints!!!" The stories we have heard are gut-wrenching, but also heartwarming. Spinal cord injuries and brain injuries don't deter the young and old from giving everything they have to get better. Every Wednesday, Thursday, and Friday for the past 11 weeks, I have seen a lot. And shared stories with patients and family members. We are like a family here. A big family. Every day we come back hoping for something big to happen. Or even small. It is very easy to get down, disappointed, or frustrated with a lack of progress. But for me, progress comes from a consistent effort every day. True in life. And Luke brings that every day. A mom came up to me today, and shared her daughter's tragic accident. She told me that her daughter loves Luke, and that she can tell how much I love Luke. So much that it hurts. Literally.

On November 2, 2016, Jenny and Luke went to the NRC for a trial run, to find out if Luke could handle walking on the Lokomat. He had a good session, and on November 7, we began our adventure at the NRC. Three days a week, every week, indefinitely. I was excited to see if this new schedule would make a difference in Luke's progress. One of us would drive to Fort Worth every Wednesday morning and return home on Friday nights. It was a challenge for our family, but we believed it was necessary for Luke.

Day one, Luke began his session on the Lokomat at 10:00 a.m. At 10:10 a.m., Luke made a sharp sound and began to tense up. The therapist immediately stopped the machine. Jenny put Luke in his wheelchair and returned to the hotel. He continued to make what sounded like muted cries for the rest of the day, night, and into the morning. The next day, Jenny took Luke to a clinic to see if it was his ear. He'd had ear infections before. But his ears were fine. She thought the therapist could just stretch Luke if he was still crying out. At 1:00 p.m., they went back to therapy. Just as the therapist began to stretch Luke on the mat, she noticed Luke's knee was swollen. Jenny then took Luke for an x-ray at Cook Children's.

Jenny called me in tears. Luke had a broken femur, the largest and strongest bone in his body. For over thirty hours Luke had cried out; he had been carried to and from the car, all while suffering from a broken femur. Luke was going to be in a cast for eight weeks. The news hit me hard. I felt angry and so sad for Luke. How much more could he take, could we take?

Something I've learned about myself is that in moments of extreme emotional stress, I react in unpredictable ways. After the news from Jenny, I grabbed my keys and my wallet and went to get a tattoo. I can't explain the thought process, but it made sense in the moment. I can't think of anyone less likely to have a tattoo than me. After the Saints won the Super Bowl in 2010, I had promised my Texas Tech tennis team that I would get a tattoo. I didn't do it. But on this day, I felt a strong urge to do something to change the vibe. I told no one. I got a fleur de lis, with Luke's name inside it, on my back. The next day, I flew to Fort Worth to be with Jenny and Luke. Jenny was surprised to see my tattoo, but she liked it.

Months passed before we revisited the idea of returning to NRC. In July of 2017, I was desperate for something positive to happen. *We need a change.* I called Bruce Conti and asked if Luke could have another opportunity to do therapy. He agreed, and in early August we had an evaluation and officially began our second try on August 22.

On Wednesdays, therapy begins at 1:00 p.m. Luke gets a Tibetan foot soak, which helps stimulate his whole body, scalp acupuncture, then a two-hour physical therapy session that ends at 4:00 p.m. In physical therapy (PT), he works on head control, stretches, and activating his muscles with stem. He finishes his session with thirty minutes on the Lokomat.

On Thursdays, Luke starts with a massage, followed by a yoga session. Kristyn does an incredible job stretching Luke, which helps his scoliosis. Luke now has a brace, which he wears only at night. After yoga, Luke spends forty-five minutes in the pool, which I believe is his favorite hour of the week. The pool his heated to 97 degrees, which warms his muscles beautifully. His last hour of the day is another session of PT and a walk on the Lokomat.

Friday is his shortest day. He gets another foot soak and scalp acupuncture, then one hour of PT. By 11:30 a.m., we are back on the road for the 350-mile trip back home.

We usually stop for a little ice cream from Chick-fil-a or Dairy Queen to finish off the week.

> **Tim Siegel, 8/23/18**
>
> One year ago today, Luke and I drove to Fort Worth to the Neurological Recovery Center for the first time. Every Wednesday to Friday the last 52 weeks. We have actually been here 46 of the last 52 weeks. I have had people ask me, "has it been worth it? Have you seen real improvement for your time there?" First of all, the NRC has helped me personally. I have time to clear my head on those long drives. I don't have the triggers that I experience in Lubbock. But more than anything, I feel HOPE when I walk through those doors. The therapists give everything they have every single day, just like they do for Luke at PTI in Lubbock. When I arrive on Wednesday and immediately see every staff member wearing their Team Luke Hope for Minds t-shirt, it makes me feel good. As I walk in the gym and everyone calls out Luke's name. Yasemin likes to call him Lukey. I am certain that Luke is improving. The Lokomat is worth the drive. The robot-

ic machine is so important as Luke is walking 80 minutes a week. My mission is to bring this to Lubbock in 2019, which will help children and adults who have Parkinson's, MS, spinal cord injuries, strokes, and brain injuries. This will also allow us to stay in Lubbock, which will be great for us and our entire family. Luke has yoga, indoor swimming, PT, and gets a massage each week. All of the caregivers feel the same way I do. The NRC gives us all hope, optimism, and we feel encouraged. I have met so many amazing families. We each share a common bond. Despite our constant struggles, we come back praying that maybe today will be THAT DAY for improvement. I am not alone. Pain lives inside all of the parents. The battles with depression, mood swings, exhaustion. But we do everything we can every day for our child. I started a support group a few months ago to help all of us. We are in a fraternity that no one envisioned. But there is a comfort that is indescribable as we share our story with each other. Next week for our support group, we will be blessed to hear from Dr. Bill Johnson, who performed

Luke's stem cell infusion. Luke has therapy from 1:00–4:00, then we will travel to
Dallas to meet with Coach Dykes at SMU
and men's tennis coach Grant Chen. One
foot in front of the other.

When in Fort Worth, I don't have the triggers that
tend to consume me when I'm in Lubbock. I don't run
into Luke's friends or see baseball fields where he played.
There are none of those memories that trigger my depression. In Fort Worth, my focus is solely on Luke, with no
distractions.

The NRC is such a special place. I think of it as a facility of hope. When Luke and I walk in the gym on Wednesday, we are greeted with "Hey Lukey," "I have missed
you, Luke," and "How is my Luke doing?" Wednesdays
is Team Luke Day and everyone wears their Team Luke
Hope for Minds shirts. The support is amazing. The therapists are young, full of energy, and give everything they
have. They absolutely love what they do. They take the
time to build relationships with their patients. I see that
every day when they are with Luke. They know he loves
the Saints, the Rangers, and Ed Sheeran. They care about
Luke. They talk to him, not about him. And it's not just
for Luke. They are the same with every patient from age
eight to eighty.

The NRC staff does as much for me emotionally as

they do for Luke. Every parent in our situation holds onto hope, it is our only option. The NRC fills me with hope from Wednesday to Friday. I feel more like the "old me" when I am there, joking around, talking sports, music, and relationships. Every time I enter the building, I am reminded that we are not the only family hurting. We are not the only family separated from our loved ones each week. We all have a story, a tragic story of spinal cord injuries, strokes, brain injuries, and other ailments.

I made it my mission to get to know the NRC families. Hearing their stories and struggles helps me find ways to offer support through Team Luke Hope for Minds. Sometimes the caretakers need their own therapy. That is why I began the Team Luke Hope for Minds support group. We meet once a month to hear speakers and to talk to each other about anything and everything. We share our thoughts and concerns, recoveries and heartbreaks. We inspire each other. We gain strength from each other.

Spencer Conti's injury in 2013 was tragic and heartbreaking. But his story, his road to recovery, and his incredible parents have helped hundreds and hundreds of families. Bruce and Lee Anne Conti could have given up, but they didn't. They also could have started a clinic just for Spencer and a few others, but they didn't. They purchased over ten million dollars worth of equipment, hired a wonderful staff, and help over 100 families every week. They took this unimaginable tragedy and turned it into a positive. For Spencer, and for so many others.

Thank you, Bruce and Lee Anne.

eleven

THE DRIVE

Every Wednesday for the last eighteen months, Luke and I headed to Fort Worth at 7:30 a.m., and every Friday we returned home around 6:00 p.m. Every week, I logged 700 miles and ten hours in the car. We have missed only a handful of weeks, for holidays and an occasional break.

I get tired, and the miles are long, but driving gives me plenty of time to reflect and to take a few deep breaths. It also gives me moments to feel sad, depressed, and helpless. Being away from Jenny and the girls for three days weighs heavily on me. And to think that my number one reason for leaving Texas Tech was so that I could spend more time with my kids. My teenage girls need their dad around, and I so much want to be there for them. I wonder if they are ones paying the highest price.

I am often asked how I do it. The answer is simple. I would do anything in the world for Luke. Yes, it has been difficult. But has it been worth it? Absolutely.

Sometimes when I stop for gas and to feed Luke, I sit with him in the back of our Dodge Promaster van. I can spend up to an hour holding him, telling him how much I love him, while trying to keep my eyes from closing. Between listening to Bruce Springsteen on satellite radio and sports talk radio on ESPN and Fox, I manage to stay awake on every trip. I would love to tell Bruce one day that in some ways his music saved my life. I never get tired of hearing his storytelling though his music. I also spend much of my time talking to the Team Luke Hope for Minds team, checking in with my friends and family, and conversing with God.

The Friday drive home is more challenging. Luke is often awake the whole way home. He is vocal, sometimes agitated, and possibly frustrated from sitting in his wheelchair the whole way home. I play classical music to help him calm down and Ed Sheeran when he is in a good mood. We talk sports. I tell him how his sisters are doing and what our plans are for the weekend. When he is agitated, I hold him because it always calms him down. He is comfortable in my arms. Sometimes I make multiple stops, and those five-hour trips turn into six- and seven-hour trips. Despite exhaustion, I have never lost patience, because I am with my boy.

Eighteen months, over 700 miles a week. Tired on Wednesday, completely exhausted on Friday. I do it for Luke. God gives me the strength.

Tim Siegel, 8/16/18

The anniversary, Luke's birthday, holidays, Luke's baseball team playing . . . those are days where I expect to feel something different. I anticipate my stomach, my head, and my heart to hurt just a little more. Conversely, there are days that hit me much, much harder than I would imagine. Yesterday was that day. I really didn't think much about the first day of school. It was a Wednesday, so that meant Luke and I were going to FW. The girls seemed ready and eager for the first day, but for me it was just another Wednesday. I thought. Luke woke up early, at around 5:00. I packed the van, got ready, told the girls I loved them, and to start off on the right foot. Jenny seemed anxious. She informed me that she had NOT slept the entire night. I gave her a big hug goodbye, and told her everything would be OK. And then the tears began pouring down. She got the words out, "I should be taking Luke to school." Luke and I got on the road around 6:30, and immediately this trip felt different. I didn't want music. I didn't even want to hear sports talk. I sat in silence. I occasionally spoke to Luke. We stopped a few times to feed and to rest. I thought and I thought some more. The funk I was in was like none other. I hurt for my girls. They need their dad. I am crushed for Jenny. I would rather break my leg than see her cry. Strangely, the trip seemed to go quicker than normal. As soon as I arrived at the NRC, and I saw all of the staff wearing their Team Luke Hope for Minds shirts, and everyone said hello to Luke . . . I felt better. The place of energy, enthusiasm, and hope. Last night I had dinner with Randall and Skip Schmidt. They opened their house to us the first nine months we were in Fort Worth. Every week, two nights a week. We have had so much given to us in so many ways, but none more generous than what they did for us. I actually stayed away from Facebook yesterday. I couldn't bear to see all of the first day of school pictures. Today is a new day. A new day for Luke to do what he does best. Fight. A new day for me. A new sprint. And I will give every ounce of energy to this hero of mine. And when I get home, I am going to wrap my arms around my girls.

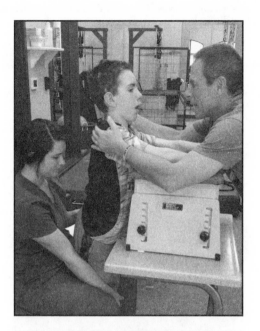

twelve

ATHLETES AND ENTERTAINERS FOR TEAM LUKE

Just days after the accident, I contacted the New Orleans Saints organization. I wanted desperately for Luke's hero, Drew Brees, to send a video to Luke. A few friends helped me reach the right person. About one month after the accident, I was sitting in our family suite at UMC when I looked down at my phone. I couldn't believe my eyes, a video from Drew.

"Hey Luke, this Drew Brees, quarterback of the New Orleans Saints. Just wanted you to know I am thinking about you buddy. Keep fighting. Hoping and praying for a full recovery. Can't wait to see you at a Saints game, in the stands cheering loud. Look forward to seeing you soon. I am praying for you."

I watched that video over and over. I smiled for the first time in a month. It was such a heartfelt message. Luke has heard that video over a thousand times. I wanted to do everything I could to stimulate Luke, to talk sports like we always did, and to let him know that so many people were praying for him. Even Drew Brees!

Everyone who knows me knows my love for the Saints. I was the tennis coach who loves his Saints. Or was it the Saints fanatic who happened to coach tennis? My players at Texas Tech knew that on Monday following a Saints loss, their practice would include more running. They all became Saints fans as well. After a big win, the team was as happy as I was, because that usually meant a lighter practice and a happier coach. What I loved more than a victory was seeing the smile on Luke's face. He was such a proud Saints fan. Like father, like son.

All of the nurses and doctors at UMC and Cook Children's quickly learned of our passion for the Saints. Room 245 at UMC and 449 at Cook had Saints decals on the door. In Luke's room, we had a Saints pillow pet, a Saints blanket, Drew Brees's book, and a Saints mascot we called Bernie. I decided in 2016 that Luke and I would keep our pact to go to New Orleans for a Saints game every year. I contacted Jay Romig, who has worked for the Saints for over forty years. I shared our story, and he agreed to show our family around the Saints facility, to let us attend practice the day before the game, and to take us on the field before the game.

On October 29, 2016, Jenny, Kate, Ellie, Luke, and I boarded a private plane for New Orleans to see our beloved team take on the Seattle Seahawks. My daughter Alex and her husband, Matt, met us there. My good friend Bobby and his two boys and Jay Lott and his family joined us as well. I was excited for them. If you haven't been to a game in the Superdome, you don't know loud. You haven't seen crazy.

Being at practice was awesome, although Luke slept through it. We were just a few feet from Mark Ingram and Brandon Cooks. As practice ended, Drew jogged over to us, took pictures with our family, spent a couple of minutes with Luke. He told him, "Hey Luke, one day I will throw you a pass." I thanked Drew and told him that next to doctors and nurses and therapists, he is the most important person in Luke's life. Drew Brees was Luke's motivation. In therapy, if Luke seemed disengaged or too tired, his therapist would play a Saints video, or just mention Drew's name. "Do it for Drew. Come on Luke, Drew wants you to move your hand. Luke, Drew loves you."

The Saints game versus Seattle was an absolute thriller. Russell Wilson's pass in the end zone fell incomplete on the last play of the game, preserving the Saints heart-pounding victory. Jenny and the girls couldn't believe the atmosphere. Unbelievably, Luke slept through the entire game.

The same weekend one year later, we were back in New Orleans, this time with two of Luke's best friends, Cole and Sam, and their dads. It was October 28, 2017, Saints vs. Bears. We were afforded the same star treatment. Practice was exciting, as there were so many former Saints players, including Jonathan Vilma, one of my all-time favorites. The boys were anxiously waiting for the end of practice, so they could meet Drew. Chase Daniel, the backup QB, came over to say that Drew wanted the last play of practice to include Luke. I wheeled Luke over to the corner of the end zone and brought Cole with him. On the last play, from the five-yard line, Drew Brees lofted a pass to the end zone, and Cole caught the pass and handed it to Luke. The team went crazy, cheering and clapping. A lot of the players came over to say hello to Luke, including Head Coach Sean Payton. The year before, Drew had promised to throw a pass to Luke, and he did, in front of the New Orleans Saints team!

Drew came up to Luke and told him that he was the Saints good luck charm. He promised Luke that if the Saints beat the Bears, he would give Luke the game ball. With less than a minute left, the Saints intercepted and held on for a 20–12 victory. A few weeks later, the game ball arrived. The game ball is in our living room.

Tim Siegel, 10/30/17

Our trip to New Orleans . . . Spending time at The Saints practice was one of the best days I have had in the last 27 months. Drew Brees had the last play of practice set up to throw the touchdown pass to Luke's buddy Cole, who then handed off to Luke. (And this was Cole's birthday.) So many of the players came up to say hello, including running back Mark Ingram, linebacker AJ Klein, and former Super Bowl Champion Jonathan Vilma. Coach Payton was so kind to spend time with us. Luke's hero, Drew Brees, is everything you want in a quarterback. A professional in every sense of the word. A leader. And a leader in the community. But his care and concern for Luke is all you need to know about Drew Brees. Today he told me that the ball used for the last play of the game will be LUKE'S GAME BALL. Luke is getting the game ball from their win over the Bears!!! Stan and Dave, two friends who have saved me from some very dark days in the last 2 years, got to see their boys at practice and on the field before the game. I loved seeing all 4 of them with big smiles. 2 fathers and their sons enjoying a once in a lifetime experience. Bittersweet for me. The truth is, I didn't really enjoy the game. I sat next to Luke, who slept the entire time. I listened to the crowd cheer for our team. I watched everyone screaming and yelling. It reminded me of me. The old me. Instead, I sat quietly hoping we would win for my boy. In the second quarter, I actually walked around with Luke because everything got to me. But at the very end, the game was close. It seems like every game in the Superdome comes down to the end. My stomach was churning. I kept thinking that we can't lose. Not with

Luke here. A few years ago, I took Luke to the Saints vs. Cowboys game, and we held hands as the Saints kicked the game winner. It was our good luck thing. As the clock was winding down, and the Saints were clinging to an 8-point lead, I grabbed Luke's hand and held it tightly. The next play, our New Orleans Saints clinched the victory with an interception. I took a deep breath and kissed Luke on the cheek.

In all of my years attending Saints games in the Superdome, I had never been to a home playoff game. Of course, there haven't been too many. The Saints hosted their divisional rival, the Carolina Panthers, on January 17, 2018. My good friend Jason Blacklock arranged for me and Luke, two of Luke's friends and their dads to fly to New Orleans for the big game. We were blessed to get to go down on the field and soak in the playoff atmosphere. The Superdome is well known for being one of the loudest stadiums. I felt like that day's game would be the loudest, craziest game I'd ever see.

I noticed Coach Payton looking over in our direction as the players were completing their warm-ups. Maybe he remembered meeting Luke just a few months earlier. What was I thinking? He was about to coach his team in a playoff game, and I was wondering if he remembered Luke. With thirty-five minutes left before kickoff, we were asked to find our seats. I had asked a security person if she would take a quick picture of all of us. As I turned to make sure Luke was looking towards the camera, out of nowhere, Coach Payton was in our picture. He had jogged over to take a picture with Luke. Amazing!

Tim Siegel, 1/8/18

If you were going to write a script for yesterday's game . . . well you couldn't. I don't have the proper words to describe all of the emotion flowing through me before, during, and after that epic win. On the sidelines, just 35 minutes before kickoff, we asked an attendant to take our picture ... and out of nowhere Coach Sean Payton joined our picture. He recognized Luke after meeting him in October. That was just the start. The atmosphere was electric. A party, New Orleans style, with 73,000 of our closest friends. Luke and I met former Saint running back Pierre Thomas during the game. I have lived through 53 years of last minute, hold-your-breath games. I held Luke's hand before the last play for good luck. Our first home

> playoff game ends dramatically with a sack of Cam Newton, and the Dome erupted. And at that very moment, Luke opened his eyes. He knew. He absolutely knew. I sent a message to Drew Brees, and he responded with, "Luke is our good luck charm." Enough said.

My stomach was churning. Nerves were in high gear. Reggie Bush led the "Who Dat" chant just before kick-off, and the crowd was in a frenzy. The Saints took the early lead, but as I have grown accustomed to watching, they could not put the Panthers away. The Panthers trailing 31-26, had the ball and were driving for the game-winning touchdown. I felt sick. My stomach was now in my throat. I kept saying to myself that the Saints couldn't lose with Luke in the building.

When the Saints were in Dallas in 2012, they lined up for the game-winning field goal. Just as they were about to snap the ball, I said to Luke, "let's hold hands for good luck." And it went through the upright. That started a mini-tradition. A huge, last-second play meant it was time to hold hands. Against the Bears just months earlier, I grabbed his hand, and what do you know, the Saints had an interception. Now with Cam Newton within striking distance, I thought about holding Luke's hand. With just a few seconds left and time for one more play, I held onto Luke's hand so tightly, and the Saints sacked Cam Newton to win! I kissed Luke on the cheek as the crowd went berserk. Maybe Luke *was* the good luck charm!

The next year, Luke and I made our annual trip to New Orleans to watch the Saints and the Cleveland Browns on September 15, 2018. I invited twelve people from Austin, Fort Worth, and Lubbock for an unforgettable weekend. Practice was awesome. Drew took pictures and signed balls and jerseys. One of the young boys in our group asked Drew if he would throw a pass. Drew threw four passes to two of the boys. The next day we all enjoyed being on the field before the game. The game was a strange affair. Low scoring with very little action, but all I cared about was getting the victory for Luke. With five seconds left, the Browns missed a game-tying field goal, and the Saints won another close one! We don't lose with Luke in the Superdome! Well, sort of. Luke and I flew to New Orleans for the Saints-Rams NFC Championship game on January 20, 2019. With five minutes left, Luke and I had to leave the Superdome to make sure we wouldn't miss our flight. As we arrived at the airport, I watched in horror as the Rams defeated the Saints in overtime. They lost, but Luke is still their good luck charm.

After the 2017 season, I contacted Drew Brees about the possibility of coming to Lubbock for our Team Luke Hope for Minds fundraising event. I knew it was a long-shot, but I know that Luke has touched his heart. Drew was always so kind to ask about Luke. Fortunately, he agreed to come. On May 9, 2018, Drew arrived and spent an hour at our house before the event. He met the rest of my family, including my dad and sister who had flown in. We talked football, of course. I mentioned that after the devastating playoff loss to the Vikings, I didn't speak to anyone in the family for two days. I was curious how he dealt with defeat. He said he had no control over the outcome, so he gets over it quickly. His response is reflective of his positive attitude towards life and football. I also mentioned that next to the birth of my children, and just above my wedding day, the Saints winning in the Super Bowl was the greatest day of my life. That made him laugh.

The event at the Lubbock Civic Center was everything we could have hoped for, and so much more. Fourteen hundred people attended! There were so many memorable moments, from Mayor Dan Pope speaking to being presented the American flag that had flown over the Capitol in Washington, D.C., thanks to Congressman Jodey Arrington.

I talked to the guests about Team Luke Hope for Minds. Two fathers spoke emotionally about their struggles with having a child who had suffered a brain injury and offered a message of hope and faith. Then Drew sat for a question and answer session. Football was only a small part of the discussion. He mostly talked about his grandfather's profound influence on his life, his faith, and he gave us wonderful, inspiring quotes to live by. Every single person in attendance was focused on his every word. Although Lubbock, Texas is Dallas Cowboys country, I imagine the New Orleans Saints are now a close second. It truly was a night to remember.

Tim Siegel, 5/10/18

I am not sure where to begin. From the second that Drew Brees came to our house to the end of the night . . . those 6 hours were the best I have felt in 33 months. The 1,400 people that came. THANK YOU from the bottom of my heart. The sponsors, our incredible volunteers, the staff at the civic center, and everyone who had a hand in this. Thank you thank you thank you. I sincerely hope everyone had a good time. Other than the lines for the food and a few mistakes on the tables, it was a nearly perfect evening. Mayor Dan Pope, Jim Archer, Bryan Mudd, and BJ Lewis . . . all of you played such a key role in the event. My amazing assistant Whitney Hoskins was simply amazing! Barney Sinclair and Harley Lopez spoke beautifully about their children. I loved seeing the standing ovation for Grayson Sparr, the 12-year-old from Rhode Island who swung 100 times a day for 100 days for Luke. Of course, I also loved everyone chanting "WHO DAT?" And finally, the MVP of the night, the hero to my Luke, and a class act in every way . . . DREW BREES. Drew spent an hour at our house talking about his family, the Saints, and our family. He talked to Luke like he had known him for years. His 30 minutes on stage was one powerful message after another. Drew Brees is the most genuine, down to earth professional athlete I have ever met. And he isn't just a professional athlete. He is the most accurate passer of all time, and sometime this upcoming season, he will be the all-time leader in passing yardage. We are talking about one of the greatest quarterbacks in the history of the NFL. And the best part . . . he is a better person than he is a quarterback. 1,400 people. Still hard to believe, especially after we had less than 2 months to prepare. Thank you for your support of the Team Luke Hope for Minds. All of your generous contributions will help children all over the country. I had one prayer yesterday. That Luke would be awake when Drew came to our house. He was. And I know he knew his hero was in our house, our city. Luke's hero truly is a HERO.

Patrick Mahomes was the quarterback for Texas Tech from 2014 to 2016. Luke and I watched him play in his freshman year, both at practice and during games. His sophomore and junior years at Tech proved that he was one of the best quarterbacks in the country. He is now the star quarterback for the Kansas City Chiefs, and the 2018 NFL MVP. Patrick has visited with Luke several times and gave him a #15 Kansas City Chiefs jersey. In 2016, the NFL launched the My Cause My Cleats initiative, where NFL players choose a nonprofit to promote by putting its logo on their cleats. In August of 2018, I received an email that Patrick Mahomes had selected Team Luke Hope for Minds as his nonprofit. How amazing is that! On December 9, 2018, Patrick Mahomes had one of his best games and led the Chiefs to a thrilling victory over the Ravens while wearing Team Luke on one shoe and Hope for Minds on the other. Those cleats were auctioned off and raised $14,300.

Luke's two favorite quarterbacks happen to be the two best of 2018, and are two of the nicest, most caring players in the league. Thank you, Drew and Patrick!

Many other athletes and celebrity figures have reached out to us to offer Luke well wishes. We will never forget Elvis Andrus of the Texas Rangers visiting Luke at Cook Children's Hospital. He has also sent Luke a few videos wishing him well. Dick Vitale, Jim Kelly, Jim Harbaugh, Donny Osmond, Terry Fater, and Dr. Phil sent their regards by video. Dick Vitale will be coming to Lubbock in 2019 to help raise money for Team Luke Hope for Minds.

We met the San Antonio Spurs in January of 2017 at a charity dinner. The entire team couldn't have been any nicer. Coach Popovich talked to Luke, while I showed Tony Parker a video of my daughter playing basketball. One point guard to another.

The tennis world has been very kind to Luke. Roger Federer, Rafael Nadal, Thomas Berdych, John Isner, Ryan Harrison, the Bryan brothers, Chris Evert, Monica Seles, Maria Sharapova, Andre Agassi, and Steffi Graf all sent beautiful messages. Brad Gilbert, Justin Gimelstob, and Mark Knowles, former tennis greats and current tennis commentators have been so supportive. Andy Roddick and Andre Agassi (who has a huge heart for children and has built schools all over the country) have both head-lined and led tennis clinics at our weekend benefit, Play for Luke, hosted each year by my friend Bobby Banck in Fort Smith, Arkansas. Thank you both, from the bottom of my heart.

All of the athletes and entertainers have meant so much to my family and me. And, I am quite certain, to Luke as well.

Tim Siegel, 10/15/17

This past weekend at the Play for Luke tennis event with Andre Agassi, I received some words of wisdom that I thought would be appropriate for others to receive. The first is to surrender to God's plan. Andre Agassi mentioned it to me, and I will always remember those words and our conversation. The word surrender has hit me hard and I know surrendering isn't easy to do, but it is a must if I want to move forward. It is easy to look back or wonder about the future but we should strive to live in the moment. My ability to live in the present is extremely important in allowing me to live the way I need to live. The second piece of wisdom I received came from a mom whose son had suffered a near fatal drowning and her advice was two simple words, "accept it." That doesn't mean to give up. Not at all. I need to accept it, and realize that every day Luke will get the best care from his therapists and so much love from his family. There is simply nothing I can do to change the past. Therefore, I have only one option. Surrender, live in the moment, and accept it. Luke and I are on the road again. Leaving now for Fort Worth so that I can speak at a school in Arlington in the morning. We will be back in time for the Cooper volleyball game Friday night vs. Monterey. That will be Team Luke Hope for Minds night.

thirteen

GOLF CART SAFETY

Writing this chapter isn't easy. I already feel an anxious-ness in my stomach as I think of the right words. I am not here to tell people to sell their golf carts or to never buy a golf cart. But I do feel that I have a responsibility to edu-cate parents on a couple of points.

Parents need to be aware of and understand the re-sponsibility they're placing on their children when they allow them to drive golf carts. The golf carts you see on a golf course are dangerous enough, but modified golf carts are faster, heavier, taller, and have a much greater chance of tipping over, which is what happened to Luke. Also, it is against the law for children to ride a golf cart on the street. It seems this isn't common knowledge based on the number of golf carts you can see in some neighborhoods. It's problematic that laws aren't consistent across states, nor are the laws enforced. Some states require the driver to be at least fourteen years old. But most states require a driver to be at least sixteen years old and have a valid driver's license. Luke was nine.

Dear Luke,

2 years ago today you had the accident in the golf cart and every single day you have had thousands of people pray for you. Do you know how proud I am of you? Before your accident, I loved watching you compete. I loved watching you with your friends. I have never seen a young boy care so much about other people. I loved how you always made sure to include everyone in your games. Remember the man who sold newspapers on that one corner? You always wanted to buy one and give him extra money. I miss watching you play Madden Football. You would yell at me to come in the room to watch the Saints destroy the Cowboys. Or when you played baseball on the Wii, and learned not to swing at the 0 and 2 count. I was so proud of you in every way. Well, except when you would occasionally run after Ellie because she made you mad. It wasn't easy to make you mad. You were the most easy-going boy in the world. Proud? So proud of you. But guess what? I am prouder of you today than ever. You have shown everyone your determination and your fight. You have taught people to pray to love, and to be closer to their families. The whole world loves you. I know they love your eyelashes! I have heard

that 1000 times! So many people have sent you videos. Drew, Elvis, Roger Federer, Nadal, and so many more. I hope you don't mind that I play you the Drew Brees video every day. Drew asked about you yesterday. He can't wait to see you when our Saints play the Bears. Remember when we used to work on ground balls over and over and over? And when you missed one, you would say "sorry Dad." I know you have days that are hard for you. Some days you are too tired, or not tired enough to fall asleep. Or you just don't feel good. But keep working hard. God is taking good care of you. You are teaching so many people so many things. Do you know that every day at least 2 people tell me they are praying for you? Some days as many as 10!!! You are my hero. I know Drew is your hero, but you are my hero. And I will be with you by your side all day every day. By the way Alex loves taking care of you. She is such a great big sis. And soon she will have a baby boy. Your Dad is going to be a grandfather. Kate and Ellie love you so much. Yes, Kate and Ellie. I remember once you asked me how I deal with those girls. I love how funny you are. Gammy comes over a lot to see you, and Matt, and a lot of your buddies think about you every day. Even when they aren't here. Your Mom is amazing. She is the boss. She does everything. Dad still isn't very handy around the house. Mom is so proud of you and loves you so so so much. Remember when

I would always say you're my boy right? And you would nod and say "yes" or "sure." I loved that more than anything. That's why I still do it today. I want you to know that you are getting better every day. And you will be talking to us very soon. Be patient. Take comfort in knowing how much we love you, how much everyone loves you, how much God loves you. Oh, I almost forgot to tell you buddy: we are going to see your favorite singer, Ed Sheeran. You and Dad. I know you love listening to his music and all of the music I play for you. But Kate thinks you don't want to hear the classical music I play for you!!! I hope you enjoy swimming with dad, and taking our walks with the dogs. Saint loves you so much. He loves to protect you. I will continue to let you know about our Texas Rangers, and everything else in sports. That's our thing. You and me. You have the whole world praying for you. That's how special you are. You are my boy my hero. I love you so much

Dad

Many kids own ATVs, golf carts, and motorized scooters. I understand that. Some parents grew up riding all kinds of motorized vehicles. Because of this, they are more likely to allow their child to ride similar vehicles at an early age. I understand that too. What I don't understand is allowing young kids to operate these vehicles without supervision. I would ask of those parents one thing: Check with

the parents of a child not your own before allowing them
to ride on or drive such a vehicle. Also, please provide helmets and safety gear for all children. We own a pool with
a cover and a trampoline with a net covering all sides. I
do not allow any child, regardless of age, to swim or jump
without first asking their parents' permission. And Jenny
or I must be home for them to play in the backyard. Safety
is always first.

Am I angry? Of course I am. This was a preventable
accident. I do realize that my anger only hurts my family,
Luke, and me. And I continue to work on moving forward, not looking back. It's a journey. My anger isn't reserved for parents who allow this behavior. It also extends
to the local police and their lack of enforcement. It is my
opinion that the police need to be more proactive in getting children in modified golf carts off the streets.

I asked a policeman in Lubbock if he witnessed two
nine-year-old boys driving a car, would he pull them over.
The answer was yes. I then asked if he saw two nine-
year-old boys driving a golf cart on a city street would he
stop them. His answer, "probably not." Even though it's
against the law. That's why parental awareness is important. Hopefully, parents in Lubbock are more aware of the
dangers because of our story.

I approached Lubbock Mayor Dan Pope about making July Golf Cart Safety Awareness Month. He thought
that was a great idea. Since 2017, I have spoken in front
of the city council sharing statistics on the golf cart injuries and reminding the community about the dangers.

The *American Journal of Preventive Medicine* reports that
injuries from golf carts surged 132 percent from 1990 to

2006. Nearly 150,000 people were hurt in golf cart accidents during that time. Each year in the U.S. about 15,000 golf cart-related injuries require emergency care. CED Technologies, Inc. first published the article "Golf Cart Accidents on the Rise" in 2012. It was revisited in 2015 and again in 2018, and not much has changed for the better.

There is no going back for my family. In a split-second, Luke's life changed, our lives changed. People have told us that it was just "kids being kids" or "boys being boys." Of course, I know that accidents happen every second of every day. But none of that matters when it is your child who's injured. I hope that Luke's accident makes parents think twice about letting their child drive on the street. Especially children under the age of fourteen. If that has happened, then some good has come out of this tragedy.

> **Tim Siegel, 12/22/15**
>
> As I lay next to Luke thinking about what our Christmas will be like for Jenny and the girls, I imagine how excited Luke would be. The last 12 days with my boy have been emotional. He has become much more agitated, even crying out for hours. But nothing I love more than trying to comfort him. I have been told that Luke's accident has brought people

closer to God, closer to their children, and has shown thousands the power of prayer. My hope is that this tragic accident also makes parents more aware of the dangers of golf carts. We as parents have the greatest responsibility in the world—to raise and protect our children. In our nearly 5 months in the hospital, we have seen many children, and heard countless stories of those who have suffered traumatic brain injuries from accidents. We live in a community where there are golf carts on the street. Some are taller, heavier, and faster than what you see on the golf course. Think twice before allowing your precious child to drive without a parent on board. Especially if your child is riding with a friend. And maybe consider wearing a helmet. Some things in life you can't control. But some are preventable. This time last year Luke and I made our bowl predictions. He wanted to win so much that he asked if he could change some of his picks— after they had already played!! Jenny and I are truly blessed to live in such a supportive community. We appreciate each and every one of your thoughts and prayers. So many people have done so much for us. I pray that each one of you has a safe and merry Christmas. Life is about moments. Some we remember more vividly than others. One moment can redirect a path forever. We trust in God that our new path is one we will cherish as a family.

fourteen

THE BRAIN BLEED

It was a nice Sunday evening on October 7, 2018. Jenny, Luke, and I had dinner with our friends Jennifer and Wayne who lived two blocks away. After dinner, Jenny left to walk Luke home and to meet our night nurse, while I stayed back to watch a little football.

Jenny left at 7:25 p.m., and literally one minute later was frantically ringing the doorbell, holding Luke awkwardly and sobbing. Luke's wheelchair had fallen over just as she was leaving their house. She had yelled and screamed but no one heard her, and she was afraid that Luke had hit his head. I carried Luke to the couch and noticed a small scrape on his right check and above his right eye. He had fallen to his right and seemed to be protected by the headrest on his wheelchair. He was alert and calm.

I put Luke back in his chair and we quickly wheeled him to our house, trying not to think the worst. Taylor, our night nurse, greeted me at the front door. I carefully put Luke in his bed as Jenny and Taylor looked him over closely. I walked to our room, sat on the bed, and took a deep breath. Was this serious? Is he ok? Thoughts flooded my brain. The picture of Jenny crying hysterically with Luke in her arms haunted me.

Jenny called me to Luke's room. They noticed that the right side of Luke's head seemed softer than normal. Jenny called Star Emergency, a small ER clinic, so that we could get a scan done as soon as possible. As we walked in the clinic, we were immediately greeted by staff. They told us they had prayed for Luke, and were honored to take care of him. Suddenly, Luke began to dry heave, and I knew something was terribly wrong. He then threw up violently.

We waited patiently for the CT scan, my stomach in knots. Jenny was blaming herself. Luke threw up again. Maybe throwing up was just a side effect of Luke hitting his head. He was still alert and calm, but I had an awful feeling. I was expecting the worst.

The doctor gave Jenny and me the bad news. Luke needed to go to Covenant Hospital's Emergency Room, immediately.

The clinic had assembled a team of first responders and an ambulance crew to transport Luke to Covenant Hospital. Luke had thrown up a third time, so it was decided that he would be intubated at Star to prevent the possibility of aspirating. Jenny rode with Luke in the ambulance. I drove with my daughter Alex, who had arrived to make sure Luke was ok. It was now 10:00 p.m., two and a half hours after the accident.

As we entered the ER at Covenant Children's Hospital, a group of twenty people, friends and family, were already waiting for us. My sweet Ellie was unable to hold back tears. Dr. Belirgen, a wonderful neurosurgeon who operated on Luke three years earlier, greeted us outside the waiting room. He broke the news that Luke had suffered a significant brain bleed on his left side, despite falling on his right side. Jenny began to cry, saying over and over that she wouldn't be able to live with herself. Dr. Belirgen drew a picture of the incision he expected to cut on Luke and assured us that it would be ok.

We went back to the waiting room by the Pediatric Intensive Care Unit as the team prepped for surgery. At midnight. Our good friend Cy Hill prayed for Luke and our family. We waited, and we waited. Three hours later, someone came in to tell us that the bleed had stopped, but that it would be another two hours before surgery was finished. Everyone had gone home by 3:00 a.m. It was only Jenny and me again; a mother and a father re-living a nightmare.

At 5:00 a.m., Dr. Belirgen came in to tell us that surgery went well, and that Luke would be moved to room seven of the PICU. It would take a day or two before we knew if the injury caused further damage. I posted an update on our Pray for Luke Siegel Facebook page, and the support and the prayers were pouring in. There were more than 1,500 comments.

On Monday morning, the waiting room began to fill up again. Visitors who had been there nearly every day three years earlier were back again. Luke's story was already on the news and online, again. Jenny and I were focused on the monitor in Luke's room, just like before. It didn't seem real, but Luke was indeed hooked up to a ventilator. His head was shaved, with a new nasty scar on the left side of his head. I wondered if my heart was ready for this again.

When the NFL schedule came out, the Saints were set to face the Washington Redskins on Monday night—week five. No coincidence that this game was scheduled for Monday night. Before the season, Drew Brees was just 1,500 yards away from breaking Peyton Manning's record for most passing yardage of all-time. He would probably break it in week five if he averaged 300 yards per game. Well here it was, Monday night football on October 8, 2018. Jenny and I had planned a big watch party at our house with six families. Luke's hero was about to break the record, and it was going to be awesome having his friends at our house. I still struggle with seeing Luke's buddies, but I wanted them at our house for this special night.

Normally, I don't like to have a lot of people around me during a Saints game. I live and die for every play. My emotions are all over the map, but I was so confident that we would win this game. Jenny and I had cleaned the house, ordered special cookies and Saints cups and plates. But all of that changed when Luke fell the night before the game. There would be no party. Far from it. I watched part of the first half in Luke's room and some in the waiting room. Thank you Drew Brees and the New Orleans Saints for lifting our spirits that night. Drew broke the record just before halftime with a touchdown pass, and the Saints dominated the Redskins. Unfortunately, I couldn't share it with Luke, as he was still heavily sedated from the surgery just fourteen hours earlier.

Luke was scheduled for an MRI on Tuesday. I was

nervous. I vividly remember what followed "based on the MRI" when the doctor gave us the diagnosis at Cook Children's three years earlier. I fully expected to hear the same thing, or maybe worse.

Dr. Nagy is a wonderful neurosurgeon. Caring, brilliant, and sympathetic. When we walked in the room to discuss the results of the MRI, I felt the same anxious "pit of my stomach" feeling. Dr. Nagy said the one major concern was the size of Luke's ventricles and the amount of fluid on his brain, which can cause pressure. A fast-acting MRI would be scheduled for Thursday to see if we needed a shunt. Another surgery. More risk of infection. *Oh God,* I thought, *please no more surgeries.*

As I listened to Dr. Nagy and looked at the images of Luke's damaged brain on the computer, I began to sink. My heart dropped. My attitude changed, but not because of the news from the MRI. We already knew the MRI would not produce good results. Now, Dr. Nagy informed us that Luke's speech and motor skills were the most affected, based on the MRI from his initial accident. The MRI doesn't measure Luke's heart and toughness and his will to fight. I know this. I have witnessed his toughness for three years. But my mood still changed so drastically. I told Jenny that I needed to go for a walk. As I walked towards the elevator, Dr. Nagy stopped me and said, "Don't you worry, you have an unbelievable fighter."

Covenant Children's Hospital was the perfect medicine for my mind and soul. I walked around the hospital and then over to the playground just south of the hospital. I had taken Kate, Ellie, and Luke there after daycare some seven years earlier. I pictured playing with all three kids, while I sat on the swing. I closed my eyes and pictured Luke on the swing right next to me. I was so deflated. So down. When I got back to Luke's room, Jenny reminded me not to focus on the MRI. The truth is, I wasn't. I was focused on what this meant for my Luke.

That afternoon, I asked Jenny to pick the girls up from school, spend time with them, and get some sleep. I wanted to stay with Luke. Three years earlier, I had been in the waiting room with friends, willing time to go by faster. I hadn't been mentally prepared to see Luke like that. This time it was different. We asked to limit visitors for fear of infection. And because I wanted to stay right next to Luke. Holding his hand and talking to him were the only things I wanted to do.

Dr. Tiva, from UMC, came by to visit Luke and, of course, he brought his ukulele. He played the same songs he had played for Luke thirty-eight months earlier. Luke's eyes flickered, and his heartrate dropped when he heard "Stand By Me." It was surreal to watch Dr. Tiva sing and play for Luke again.

Tim Siegel, 10/5/16

> Today I felt my chest was going to explode. I honestly thought about going to the ER because of the anxiety and stress I felt following my 2 tennis classes at Laura Bush. I decided to take a walk

on the track right next to the courts. I desperately needed to clear my head. Minutes before, I checked on Luke and saw that he wasn't responding to therapy. I couldn't have been more down at the moment. I walked on lane 3 and tuned on the Eagles on Pandora. Here is where I think there was a sign. Or I am just over-thinking. First song, "Take it to the Limit." I felt like I was at the limit. Second song, "Go Your Own Way." I feel like sometimes I am going my own way, which scares me. Third song, "Running on Empty." My tank feels empty. Fourth song, "Still the Same." God knows I don't feel or act the same. And as I got in my car, I turned on the radio to . . ."Beautiful Day," Our wedding song. The pain that I feel some-times hits me so hard that it is difficult to breathe. I know that I am physically exhausted. And just as tired emotionally. When you think of the same thing every minute of every day for 14 months . . . Luke loves music too. We play his favor-ite songs all the time. I know he enjoys it. He is just like his Dad.

I am a light sleeper. Always have been. Sleeping on a couch three feet away from Luke, and ten feet away from the nurses' station, and five feet away from the monitors, you can imagine how much I slept. For the first two years after the accident, I didn't sleep a full night. I was so programmed to wake up and turn Luke, even after we hired a night nurse to care for Luke. Once I'm up, it's nearly impossible for me to fall back asleep.

In the last year, I have managed to get eight straight hours of sleep at night, and it has been more than a blessing. My moods are better, my energy is better, and my outlook is definitely better. I owe it all to the amazing staff of nurses we have at home. Astrid has been Luke's night nurse for three years. She is Luke's angel. Two or three nights every week, Astrid stays with Luke, loves on him, talks to him, and holds him close to her heart. We appreciate everything she has done for Luke. She is part of our family. Taylor joined us in 2018, staying at night on an as-needed basis. She is so caring, professional, and loving. We have Amanda twice a week, on Mondays and Tuesdays, during the day. She is wonderful with Luke, always cheering him on at therapy.

Luke had a fast-acting MRI on Thursday afternoon, and the doctors said that a shunt was not necessary. Thank God, because Luke didn't need another surgery and Luke was cleared to go home the next day.

Tim Siegel, 10/15/18

Now that we have been home for a few days, I have had an opportunity to reflect on the last week. It is so hard to believe that Luke had a 5-hour surgery for a significant brain bleed exactly one week ago, and then we came home 5 days later. So much went through my mind those 5 days. I am still worn out emotionally. Seeing my wife and girls so upset will forever be etched in my memory. Watching the brain pressure numbers on the monitor over and over and over was what I did for months after the accident. I seemed to focus on that the first couple of days last week as well. I want to say a huge thank you to the Covenant Staff. Every member of the staff was terrific. I have always had such admiration for nurses and doctors, and after last week, even more. Dr. Belirgen and Dr. Nagy will always have a special place in my heart. They both were there for Luke 3 years ago and again last week. They are well-respected neurosurgeons, and even better people. Dr. Nagy is an opera singer, and stunned us all as he sang to Luke last Thursday. He knew Luke loves music. A special moment for all of us. I was reminded last week that so many families deal with pain, unbearable pain. If each of us spent 5 minutes a month in a hospital visiting, I don't think we would take as much for granted as we do. Jenny and I saw Luke's MRI on Thursday, and heard how it hasn't changed. He shouldn't be making a sound or using his limbs. I walked out of the hospital on that Thursday down. Sad. Depressed. As I was walking, I said to God, *if Luke doesn't need a shunt I will run every day.* He didn't need one. So, if you see me feel free to encourage me, or better yet, hold me accountable! We thank God that Luke is home. We plan to ease into therapy this week, and will be back in Fort Worth next week. If you look at his head, his scars from 3 years ago, and from last week look like he has a 'T' and 'C' shaved into his scalp. My daughter Kate said it best when she revealed that those initials stand for Tough Cookie. I showed Dr. Nagy videos of Luke trying to speak, moving his foot, and working on head control. His response was perfect. "You have one unbelievable fighter."

Amen.

The weekend was uneventful. Luke was still throwing up, but we think it was because he resumed his neurotransmitter, which he had gone six days without. On Monday, we took Luke to occupational therapy. He immediately threw up when I put him on the mat for his session. He did some stretching but did not respond at all. In speech therapy, he wouldn't swallow. This scared me. Was he back to square one? Will he have to learn how to swallow all over again?

Our day nurse, Amanda, noticed that Luke had more swelling on his head. Less than two hours later, we were at UMC meeting with Dr. Nagy. He asked us to come back the next day if the swelling increased. Tuesday morning was worse. Amanda and I took Luke to Covenant Children's ER. Dr. Belirgen performed an aspiration to drain the fluid from Luke's head. He took out 110 ml of fluid— two syringes! He then wrapped Luke's head and asked that we come back in two days. By Thursday, he looked good. The shunt or a lumbar puncture were still possibilities, but as of now we were on the road to healing.

By then, Luke had gone two weeks without therapy. *How much of a setback were we facing? Was the injury worse than we thought?* The upside of being at home the last two weeks was that I had more time with Jenny and the girls. These two weeks were terrifying and so hard on all of us. Seeing Jenny and the girls so emotional was all I could handle. But thank God, this chapter is behind us. Now we wait, hope, and pray that Luke will get to his baseline soon.

fifteen

THANK YOU, TEXAS TECH

I coached at Texas Tech from January of 1993 to August 2015, for twenty-three wonderful years. Coaching was a big part of my job, but the relationships I had and still have with my players are more special than any trophy. The Texas Tech coaches I worked with have all become family. My kids knew if there was a Texas Tech sporting event, and my tennis team wasn't competing that day, then we were going to cheer on whatever team was playing. We watched every sport including: football, basketball, baseball, soccer, softball, women's basketball, a track meet, and volleyball. I am a sports fan; therefore, I want to watch all sports. But I am also a friend to those coaches. When I arrived in the morning, I started on one side of the building and talked to every coach and staff person I saw. We loved the comradery.

Texas Tech Athletics has become an elite athletic department. Athletic Director Kirby Hocutt has done a terrific job in every area. Our facilities are as good as any in the country. The budgets have improved dramatically. The support staff is outstanding. The coaching staff to this day are still dear friends of mine. I send a group text showing videos of Luke in therapy to all the coaches every week. I supported and cheered on their teams. Today they all support and cheer on Luke and me. It is impossible to put into words my appreciation when they include him in special events. This year Luke "threw" the first pitch in softball and in baseball. He was introduced at a soccer game, volleyball game, Lady Raider basketball game, and at a tennis match. He received a standing ovation from a crowd of 60,000 people at a Texas Tech football game. Kliff Kingsbury, the former Texas Tech football coach, cares about Luke so much; he invited us several times to attend practice, and the entire team would say hello to Luke. Kliff means so much to the Lubbock community, and he will always mean so much to our family.

Tim Siegel, 3/1/18

One of my proudest moments. Luke was 5 when he threw out the first pitch at the Texas Tech vs. Texas baseball game. This Saturday, March 3, Luke will once again "throw out" the first pitch at the Texas Tech baseball game.

Chris Beard is the men's basketball coach at Texas Tech. He took Texas Tech to an Elite Eight appearance in only his second year. He is one heck of a basketball coach, but his coaching doesn't compare to what he means to Luke and me. At a young age, Luke absolutely loved watching Red Raider basketball. When the kids were little, Alex and the three little ones would sit right in the front row, often showing up on the big screen. Chris has invited Luke and me to practices and we even got to spend time with the team the day before the NCAA Championship. In the 2018 season, ESPN College Gameday came to Lubbock for the Texas Tech vs. Kansas game. That morning, we watched the game from home and were surprised to see every Texas Tech player wearing a Team Luke Hope for Minds t-shirt.

On November 24, 2018, we were invited to the locker room after a big win. One of the players prayed for Luke, and then one by one each player gave Luke a hug. Heart-warming. Coach Beard is teaching his players much more than the game of basketball.

Tim Siegel, 11/24/18

Luke and I went to the Texas Tech basketball game, and after our big win we were invited to the locker room. This was very touching. Each player went up to Luke and gave him a hug. The love they had for Luke is heart-warming. We appreciate the support from Coach Beard, the entire staff, and the team.

Thank you, Texas Tech, for twenty-three glorious years. Thank you, Kirby Hocutt, the Athletic department staff, and all of the coaches and student athletes who have prayed for and supported Luke. I know he knows. Thank you.

sixteen

MY FRIEND BOBBY

Now that I am fifty-five years old, I have a much better grasp of what it is really important in life. Age has helped me figure this out. Luke's accident helped put things into perspective as well. But the one thing I have always known—at fifteen, twenty-five, thirty-five, and now at fifty-five, is that friendships are very important to me. I have been blessed throughout my life with very special friendships. After Luke's accident, I lost a few friends, but some of my closest friends today are people I met because of the accident.

The world would be a better place if every person in the world had one true loyal friend, who doesn't judge and who has seen the best and the worst in you—a friendship that has gotten stronger over the years. Well, I have that friend in Bobby Banck.

Bobby and I met in 1976, across the net at the Boys 12 Nationals in the finals of doubles. Bobby was born in Buffalo, New York, but moved to Bradenton, Florida at the age of thirteen so that he could train at the prestigious Nick Bollettieri Tennis Academy (now IMG Academy). He and I played the same national junior tournament throughout the years. When it came time to choose a college where we would continue our tennis career, Bobby chose the University of Arkansas over Tennessee. I was so close to attending Clemson but decided to join Bobby and become a Razorback as well. We traveled the world together on the professional tour. After retiring, Bobby coached Monica Seles, Mary Joe Fernandez, Aaron Krickstein, and others.

We speak on the phone nearly every day. We probably haven't gone more than three or four days without talking since college. Despite living in different states, we see each other a couple of times a year. Bobby now lives in Fort Smith, Arkansas with his beautiful wife and two sons. We have been there for each other, we were each other's best man at our respective weddings, and we encourage each other when things get challenging.

The day after Luke's accident, Bobby drove nine hours to visit Luke in the hospital and to stay with us for a few days. He made the same trip six or seven times, sometimes staying only twenty-four hours. I imagine that seeing Luke touches fathers of sons in a deeper, more visceral way. Luke is almost like Bobby's third son. And I'm certain Bobby has pictured that same thing happening to his boys.

Bobby is now the president of Team Luke Hope for Minds. He joins every board meeting, either by call or in person. Bobby's heart is as big as anyone's I have ever met. No one is more giving and generous and caring. His passion to help spread awareness about our nonprofit is only matched by his concern for Luke.

Bobby is the tennis director of Hardscrabble Country Club and knows a group of ladies who love tennis and want to help us in any way. In September of 2016, Bobby organized the first Play for Luke event, a benefit for our family. He brought in legendary tennis coach Nick Bollettieri to run adult and junior clinics. There was a dinner the night before, an auction, and fantastic day of tennis. Former professional tennis players flew in from all over the country. The event raised over $100,000. The next year, Andy Roddick headlined. It was getting better and better each year. In September of 2018, Bobby outdid himself. Andre Agassi, one of the greatest tennis players of all time, came to Fort Smith, Arkansas and helped us raise over $200,000. Bobby and his amazing group of volunteers put on a cocktail party, clinics with Andre, and an evening concert. It was such a spectacular event that clearly took months to plan.

Bobby Banck has been one heck of a friend since we were twelve years old, but since the accident it's impossible to put into words what he means to me and our family. I honestly don't know if I could have gotten through the last three and a half years without his friendship, support, and encouragement. And his heart of gold.

seventeen

OUR FAMILY,
THEN AND NOW

Prior to July 28, 2015, our family was doing well and looking forward to my career transition. I had resigned from Texas Tech on July 8 and was fired up to spend more time with my children. I was excited about doing things with my kids that I had been unable to do while I was coaching.

Tim Siegel, 7/7/18

> I take an anti-depressant. I see a therapist. This weekend I have found a new medicine and therapy. Watching my Kate play basketball with her AAU Team has been just what I needed. Kate and I have had a great time together, along

with Jenny's brother and his family. This does feel like it used to feel. I'm trying to be the old Tim ... getting the girls fired up, while cheering with all of the parents. Just like old times. I have called Jenny 100 times to check on Luke. I think about him constantly. But I have focused on enjoying this weekend, the team, the families, and most of all, #3 Kate Siegel. The team has won 3 games and will play in the semi-finals tomorrow morning. Kate and I have watched the World Cup, Wimbledon, NBA Summer League, and shopped at the mall. It is easier for me to be me when I am not in Lubbock. Fewer triggers. 17 years ago today, Jenny and I got married at the Broadmoor in Colorado Springs. The MVP of our family is home with Luke and Ellie. I couldn't have survived these last 3 years without her. I thank God for her and all that she does to keep our family moving forward. I am trying so hard not to look back. If I do, I am not able to put one foot in front of the other.

The month of March is a very busy time for college tennis, but in high school there are no matches over spring break. Luke and I had planned to go to Arizona every spring break to watch spring training games. When I first told him this, you should have seen the smile on his sweet face. Ellie had cheer competitions late fall through early spring. I had only been to a couple of them. Now, I would get to watch Ellie cheer. Kate played basketball and volleyball throughout the year. I was excited for the opportunity to watch her middle school games, her AAU games, as well as club and school volleyball.

It wasn't just the sporting events I could now attend. It was being at home, having dinner with the family, and helping Jenny, which was something she deserved after my fourteen years of traveling as a college coach. Jenny oversees so much at our house. She handles bills, and all the insurance stuff, and she is handy around the house. I am not sure what I add, although I like things neat and I do my fair share of laundry. Jenny enjoys her cup of coffee and reading the news on her phone. I, on the other hand, have never had a cup of coffee, and the only real escape for me is watching sports. The one thing I can count on to make me smile is watching *Seinfeld*. I am the biggest *Seinfeld* fan on the planet. My other escape, or therapy is my walks around the neighborhood with our dogs, Saint and Jerzey. But honestly, my escape, and my therapy, and my favorite thing is to be right by Luke.

Tim Siegel, 6/16/18

Father's Day. These 4 children of mine mean the world to me. For me, every

day is Father's Day. There is nothing I
would rather do than to be with my kids.
Being a father is the greatest responsibility in the world, and I don't take that
for granted. It is what gives me such
great joy. I vividly remember traveling
with the Texas Tech tennis team when
Alex was a little girl, and I couldn't wait
to get home to be with her. She lived
with me while her mom fought a brave
battle with diabetes. Her mom passed
away in 2004. I loved to leave notes for
the 3 little ones when I was traveling. I
hated to be away from them. And how
I loved the hugs after a long trip. The
tough losses always felt better when
they were in my arms. The last trip we
all took together was June of 2015. Alex
and Matt's wedding in Las Vegas. Just 7
weeks before Luke's accident. I learned
a lot from my dad, the smartest and most
patient man I have ever met. At 85, he is
as sharp as ever. Father's Day. Today,
I think about Father's Day a little differently. Tomorrow will be my 3rd Father's
Day since Luke's accident. Some dads
may identify who they are based on what

they do for a living. I always saw myself
not as tennis player or coach, but as a
dad. Today more than ever. We all know
being a parent has its many challenges,
especially in the time of social media.
But there is nothing more rewarding than
to be a parent. I saw a beautiful family
today while I was getting Luke a haircut.
3 boys and mom and dad. So happy.
I found myself just watching the father
talk to his sons. Today, Jenny and I did
something we haven't done in 3 years.
We took Kate, Ellie, and Luke to see *The
Incredibles.* I watched Luke look at the
screen with his headphones on, wondering what he knew, what he could see,
and it was all I could do to not wrap my
arms around him. We all say the same
thing. We can't believe how time flies.
How quickly they grow up. So, to all dads
out there. Enjoy every moment with your
children. No career, no amount of money,
nothing is more important than the quality
time you spend with your children. Invest
in what they are doing, who their friends
are, how they are doing in school. I left
Tech so that I could spend more time with

my kids, but since August, I am gone with Luke 3 days a week. That eats at me every day. I also know that there are days that I am here in the house physically, but not emotionally. So, tomorrow is a reminder for me to try to be the best dad I can be, despite our struggles. To focus on all of my children. To continue to give Luke my heart and soul. And to be the best husband I can be to my wife. Happy Father's Day.

Seven weeks before the accident, my eldest daughter, Alex, married her high school sweetheart, Matt, in a beautiful ceremony at Mandalay Bay in Las Vegas. That wonderful weekend was the last time the whole family was together prior to the accident. Alex was born in 1992 in Dallas while I was coaching at SMU. Alex's mom, Laura, and I divorced in 1995 after five years of marriage but remained close friends. On November 2, 2004, I received the devastating news that Laura had passed away at the age of thirty-nine. Laura had battled diabetes since 1990. Alex came to live with me full time after her mom passed. I did the very best I could raising her, but when I look back at pictures of Alex's hair and her clothes, I probably could have used more help.

After Laura passed away, Alex decided she wanted to

be a nurse so that she could help people who were going through similar struggles. Alex went through a lot after her mom and Matt's mom passed away. I probably will never understand how bad it was for her. But she took that pain and used it to help others.

Today, Alex is a registered nurse. She helped take care of Luke for over two years, and is currently working for an infertility doctor in Lubbock. I am very proud of the daughter and mom Alex is and the woman she has become. She and Matt blessed our family with my grandson, Tommy, born on November 4, 2017. He may be the happiest baby in the world. He has been the light that our family needed. I didn't think I could love another little boy the way I love Luke, until Tommy came along. Tommy has captured something inside of me and brought me more joy than I ever knew I had. He can put a smile on my face on even my darkest days. He is so cheerful and makes me forget about all the sadness. I do often wonder how I will feel when he is old enough to throw a football or baseball.

Kate turned sixteen in January 2019. She has been a terrific athlete and basketball player from a very early age. She has played on the West Texas Breeze AAU team since third grade. Today, she is the point guard for her high school team. She's also the libero on her high school volleyball team. I am proud of Kate's competitive spirit and her IQ in both sports. Kate and I enjoy talking about and following the NBA and the Saints, and I love watching games with her. When she isn't competing, she's spending time with little Tommy (her love for him is beautiful to see) and watching *Grey's Anatomy*, *Friends*, and *Criminal*

Minds. She is wise beyond her years. She's not comfortable expressing herself when it comes to Luke's accident, but I see the pain, and hurt, and occasional anger. When she turns eighteen, she wants to get a small tattoo of something Luke wrote.

Ellie, fourteen, is our cheerleader. She was part of a competitive cheer team for a few years and spent countless hours practicing with her team. She is a fearless tumbler. She also plays volleyball, and her eighth-grade team won the city championship in 2018. Ellie is our quick-witted, spunky, little fireball who loves to keep us on our toes. She enjoys spending time with her friends. She wears her emotions on her sleeve more than Kate and is also aware that she needs to be more talkative with Luke.

My girls are so special, and I am proud of each of them. Luke's accident has been tragic for them too. Alex, Kate, and Ellie lost the brother they knew. And they had to form a new relationship with a brother who is so different. That's not easy for young children to understand. But my girls have been amazing throughout this journey. They've been patient, understanding, and forgiving. I couldn't ask anything else of them.

On December 19, 2018, I gave myself the best Christmas present—quality time with my girls. Kate, Ellie, and I flew to New York City to see Pentatonix on Broadway and to watch our Texas Tech Red Raiders take on the Duke Blue Devils in Madison Square Garden. And we capped the weekend by flying back on the team plane. What a beautiful time with my girls. We need more of this for sure.

Tim Siegel, 6/26/17

During these last 23 months, my girls have gone through so much. They tend to be the forgotten ones. They haven't gotten as much attention from me as they would have liked. And it absolutely kills me. They haven't had a conversation with Luke in 23 months. And every day they are asked how Luke is doing. But I wonder how often they are asked how they are doing. Kate made this very special tribute to Luke. This video is set to a Bruce Springsteen song called "Tougher Than the Rest." Nobody tougher than Luke.

My wife is beautiful inside and out. I find her more beautiful today than on the day we got married, July 7, 2001. I admire and respect her for the wife she is, and the wonderful mom she has been to Alex and our three young ones. She's incredibly hard working, both at home and working as a nurse practitioner. Our family was a loving, happy, active family. I loved coaching at Texas Tech, but I wanted less travel and spend more time with the kids. I couldn't wait for the next chapter in our lives. Before the accident, our kids looked forward to summer vacations, loved watching Texas Tech sporting events, and generally enjoyed being around each other.

We have so many wonderful family memories, it's hard to pick a favorite. There's the time we were at a Texas Rangers game, and a Toronto Blue Jay player handed Kate a ball. Our trip to Disney World in 2012, when we put toilet paper in Luke's shoes so he would be tall enough to ride the roller coaster with his sisters. In hindsight, not the best parenting move. There were our trips to New York City to see Broadway shows and Times Square. And the time our entire family cheered on my tennis team as we played Texas in a night match, with over a thousand people in the stands. We pulled out the historic match. We took a family picture on court two. I remember our family all watching Kate play basketball, and being at the baseball fields cheering on sweet Luke. And I remember my entire family all gathered in my office on games days, especially on November 1, 2008, when we witnessed the greatest night of Texas Tech football, the epic win over Texas.

Since July 28, 2015, our family has not been the same. I am not the same. Before the accident, life was good. I was a positive person with a wonderful family and a great job. I never battled depression, anxiety, and mental health issues, but I had sympathy and understanding for those who did. I've seen it firsthand with my older brother.

But I've changed. Now my moods are all over the map. My energy level. My sleeping. My motivation. All of it. It's incredibly difficult to juggle the demands of our non-profit, the travel to Fort Worth every week, giving my girls the time and attention they deserve, and being as good of a husband as possible. And of course, taking care of

Luke. I desperately want to keep our family close, to stay positive and healthy, and to be a leader and role model for my girls.

Not too long ago, Jenny sat me down for a kind of intervention. She said that I was numb to everything around me, except Luke. It was a punch in the gut. But I needed to hear it. Being present for her and the girls is incredibly important, but I always feel my priority is to be with Luke.

The stress of it all, and the constant worry about what's next, takes a toll emotionally and physically. As a coach, I have always been able to fix, to teach, to coach, to develop, to improve. I can't get the results for Luke that I used to be able to get from my team, at least not as quickly. But I'll never stop trying.

With the help of medicine, talk therapy, and my family, I do believe I am on the right track. My days are better than they were last year, and the year before that. My anger comes and goes now, it's not with me every day like it used to be. I have faith that I will continue to get better. I also have faith that Luke will get better. They say that time heals. I'm waiting. I suppose I will be waiting until I take my last breath.

Throughout all of this, Jenny and I started to feel like we are just roommates. We sleep in different beds four nights a week, as one of us is in Luke's room when the night nurse isn't there. We are a good team and are doing everything we can for our girls and Luke. But our marriage isn't the same. It's not bad, just not the same. How could it be? Fortunately, we receive regular counseling. We both are in pain, and we need each other more now than ever. We couldn't do this without the other. Jenny is my rock. She is so strong. I admire her so much. I hate to see her in pain, but there are times I can't help her because my own pain is overwhelming.

And our girls are going through tough times. When the accident happened, Kate and Ellie were twelve and ten. Now they are sixteen and fourteen, and they understand the severity much more clearly. They have their own unresolved feelings and emotions about the accident, about Luke's health, about the sacrifices they make. But I've noticed that since the accident, my girls are more compassionate and more patient. They notice people with special needs more now than ever. That make me happy. Still, they both have a hard time talking to Luke, beyond a pleasant greeting. It's more of a "hey Luke" than actually talking to him. They are uncomfortable sitting with Luke and just telling him about their day. They wonder if Luke even knows who they are, and if he even understands, which makes Jenny and me especially sad. Alex has been a supportive sister to Kate and Ellie, always there to help them through the hard moments—even as she tries to balance being a nurse and starting a family of her own.

Kate and Ellie both hate the attention, whether it's someone stopping us at a restaurant or people asking them about Luke. They are never asked how they are doing. It's always "how is Luke doing?" They hurt and sometimes are scared but aren't comfortable showing their emotions. Kate keeps things inside and deals with more anger than Ellie, while Ellie is more likely to shed a tear. I will work every day to be there for them, to talk to them, to help them. Our family will be ok. I know that. Our family dynamic has changed, but our love for each other hasn't.

eighteen

DEAR PARENTS: A LETTER OF HOPE

Those who think there is a time limit when grieving . . . have never lost a piece of the heart.

O ver the last three and a half years, I have been through a lot. And I have seen a lot. There are so many families going through similar situations. God knows it isn't easy. At times, moving forward feels impossible. Day after day, week after week, hoping for improvement. But one of the many things I have learned is that without hope and faith, there is absolutely no way I could survive. Hope has become one of the most important words in my vocabulary. Without hope, without faith, we have nothing.

Surrender to what is, let go what was. Have faith in what will be.

So many families in similar situations were given little hope, but we must never give up. I have visited with parents who were told emphatically that their child would never talk, never use their limbs, and that the rest of their life should be spent in a nursing home. And yet, these children are improving. And remember, there will be setbacks, there will be weeks of very little improvement, but it will come. Be patient.

I am here to tell all of you that as wonderful as our doctors have been, and as bad as Luke's last MRI was, I choose to believe that Luke will improve. I have no doubt in my mind. Remember, an MRI can't measure your will to fight or how hard you work. I am 100 percent convinced that consistent therapy has helped Luke more than anything. Physical therapy, occupational therapy, and speech therapy are crucial to his progress.

The coach in me believes in pushing Luke as much as he can handle. Luke needs sleep, and he needs rest, but sitting in his chair or lying in bed for extended periods will not produce results. Your child's muscles need to be stretched and massaged constantly. When tone kicks in, Luke's upper body and arms get extremely tight. I would imagine it feels like a cramp. Luke also has had aquatic therapy, hippotherapy (horse), music therapy, yoga, and massages, including cranial sacral. Some of the treatments we've tried are quite expensive, but some families have seen results. He has had forty hyperbaric oxygen treatments, which is extremely popular for children who have suffered a brain injury. It has produced results in movement and alertness for some children. He's also had three stem cell infusions. Which therapies and treatments work best for Luke? I have no idea. Every patient is different. Results are different as well. Jenny and I are open to trying different procedures as often as we can. Even if it means we need to downsize at some point. A house is just a house, right? But what I do know is that I want to give Luke every opportunity for improvement by exposing him to everything.

My teenage girls need to be motivated in school and athletics, and Luke is no different. We have no idea what his potential is, but I will never stop trying to find out how far he can go. He has progressed far more than our doctors had predicted. Every day it seems that someone sends me a supplement to try, or a new piece of equipment I should consider. I am all for researching everything.

The groups I have found on Facebook for brain injuries are a great way to get information about what works, and most importantly they offer opportunities to be there for each other. We are not alone. I know it feels that way when friends are enjoying their family vacations or sharing updates about their fun holiday. I hurt when Luke's friends are playing sports. It feels like my insides are being ripped out. It does Luke no good when I live in the past, and does me no good when I worry about the future. This is our life now, Luke's life now, and I will do my very best to make the most of it.

Don't ever give up hope and faith. I've had many emotional nights when I wondered if we would ever see improvement. But I believe with all my heart that with love, therapy, hope, and faith, Luke will continue to make strides. Yes, small strides, very small, but it's still progress.

This isn't the life we or anyone expected or imagined.

I constantly remind myself what I told Jenny just weeks before the accident, "Luke will make an impact on so many people. He has a tender heart and a sweet soul." Well, he sure is impacting people. Hope and impact are my new favorite words. Luke's impact is far-reaching, and I must never forget that. Your child can have a similar impact as well.

The same difficult news I hear from doctors is the very thing that gives me optimism. The MRI is a gauge, but that's all it is. You treat the patient, not the MRI. The MRI can't measure Luke's heart and desire to improve. They don't know how much better Luke can be. They simply don't know. I think about the tennis player I had who had average athletic ability, his strokes weren't pretty, he didn't move well, so he wasn't supposed to be good. But he knew how to win because of his toughness, his heart, and his competitiveness. I approach Luke's progress the same way: you can't measure Luke's fight, his toughness, his heart, and his will to get better.

The road is bumpy at best. For a short time, everything will be going smoothly, then all of a sudden, you're dealing with infection, constipation, or any number of things that can happen. Just stay the course, despite the setbacks. We certainly have had our share. Don't ever stop praying. Believe in miracles. And you'll begin to see better days.

I believe with all my heart that Luke understands. He feels my presence. I think he is trapped in his body, so desperate to come out. But he knows how much I love him.

I have been told a hundred times, "You have to take care of yourself so that you can take care of Luke." I know. I know. I know. I do sleep better, but I tend to eat poorly when I am overly tired. I have gained over fifteen pounds since the accident, mostly from a lack of exercise. I used to be disciplined as an athlete and as a coach. Exercise has been a major part of my life since I was six years old. For the past three and a half years, not so much. I am working towards getting fit again, physically and emotionally.

I am also taking better care of myself emotionally, as I see a therapist every Monday. This has been good for me on so many levels. For me, for Jenny and our marriage, and for Luke. He needs me at my best. He also needs me to laugh, go to dinner with friends, and take time for a trip with Jenny. He also needs me to enjoy my time with the girls.

Luke's accident was devastating. I still can't believe this is our life now. I still wake up thinking it was a bad dream. But it does me no good to look back, and no good to worry about the future. I have to remind myself to stay in the moment and do everything I can for Jenny, the girls, and for Luke. This new sprint, or new marathon every day may leave me winded and gasping for air, but it won't stop me.

In November of 2018, two people said the same thing to me just minutes apart from each other: "God is using you to impact and inspire others." And maybe that is true. I know Luke is an inspiration to so many. I am just trying to help my son and others who are going through devastating injuries, illness, or the death of a loved one. This road we are on is a painful one. If I can help someone survive by spreading messages of hope and faith, then maybe, just maybe, Luke and I are being used by God to impact others.

I enjoy offering advice, encouragement, and information to parents and families and encourage anyone to contact me. My email is tim@teamlukehopeforminds.org. Resources are available on the Team Luke Hope for Minds website, teamlukehopeforminds.org. You can find out about upcoming events, and visit our store to purchase Team Luke merchandise. And if you're interested, please help us spread the word and bring awareness to traumatic brain injuries.

Tim Siegel, 12/13/18

I love how much Jenny loves Christmas. She has a small tree in all of our bedrooms, and just loves this time of the year. But it certainly doesn't feel like it used to feel. Not for her, and not for me. When I hear someone say "Merry Christmas," sometimes I wonder if it will ever be Merry. I am not alone. Such a joyous time of the year for some, and yet the most painful time of the year for others. With pain also comes anxiety, panic attacks and overwhelming stress. Yesterday, I was talking to someone at the NRC, and she said that nearly everyone in here deals with post-traumatic stress. It's real. My wonderful wife suffers from panic attacks, and a tremendous amount of anxiety. So hard for me to watch. This started just 2 months after the accident. I hope that all of you who are in "pain" at this time of the year, or those who suffer from anxiety, can find peace and comfort. Don't hesitate to get help. One foot in front of the other.

nineteen

LUKE AND
THE FUTURE

Tim Siegel, 7/28/18

"Luke has been in an accident."
"Are you serious, how bad is it?"
"I think he broke his nose."
Those were the words spoken on July
28, 2015 at 2 p.m. 3 years ago today.
1,095 days ago. They say time heals.
Maybe in some way time has helped me
realize that I can't go back in time. I hurt.
I literally feel my stomach as I write this
morning, but I do understand that I have
a responsibility to be the best husband
to Jenny and be there for my 3 girls. I
am aware that if I don't take care of me, I

won't be able to take care of Luke. I say this as my lower back is tight from holding Luke last night. I am aware that Luke has made progress. I was on my phone last night going through my thousands of pictures. Some from the first few days, and others from our days at Cook Children's. His features have changed obviously, but his ability to move his eyes, and show expression were nonexistent 3 years ago. I am aware that my attitude is crucial in my improvement. I have gotten better. The better days are better, but the difficult days seem worse. I am seeing a therapist every Monday without fail. Jenny and I are going to try to take at least one day per month for us. NYC was so good for us. I am aware that my 2 beautiful teenage girls need their dad more than ever. I am aware that although my moods fluctuate dramatically, I need friends more than ever. I am aware that this journey will take years, the rest of our lives. I am going to continue to give everything I have to help Luke. Every ounce of my being. I am aware that without my faith, I don't know if I could keep going. I am certain that I would be in a hospital or worse without my faith. Time has also brought me to the realization that Luke's story has changed lives. Thousands of lives. So many stories of parents loving their children differently, and children praying and showing compassion. Famous people have shown their love. Professional tennis players, Elvis Andrus of the Texas Rangers, and, of course, Drew Brees. I still find it hard to believe that Drew Brees came to our house and spoke in front of 1,400 people to help our organization. Team Luke Hope for Minds. Luke's accident gave me the purpose, the passion, and the calling to help other children who have suffered a brain injury. We have given out over $150,000 to help families all over the country. We have helped hundreds of others through counseling, support groups, and education. I visited a beautiful family in Dallas on Wednesday, whose daughter suffered a brain injury less than 2 years ago. I have spoken in front of thousands of students, and this year will stand in front of thousands more. Helping others has helped me. I decided to post the beautiful song Brandon Gwinn wrote and sang called "My Boy (Luke's Song)." It has it all. Beautiful words and pictures of Luke then and now. Today is hard, but I am not sure if it is any harder than any other day. Thank you all for being with us for the last 3 years.

Three and a half years after Luke's accident, and the question I get often is, "So, what do the doctors think Luke's recovery will be?" I wish I knew. Oh God, Jenny and I would love to know.

I think about a friend of mine whose son didn't speak for six years, and then one day he began to mumble words together. Will Luke ever say words? He does respond to me, just not verbally. At therapy, we ask Luke to kick the ball with his right foot, occasionally his right foot will move. Not his left, but the correct foot. That is no coincidence.

One of the many things that keeps me up at night is wondering what Luke is thinking. *Is he scared? Is he mad? Is he more aware of his situation today than he was six months or one year ago? Does he ever think, "if this is my life forever, I don't want any part of this"? Does his mind allow him to go back to the day of the accident?* When Luke makes sounds, I wonder, *is it his stomach or does he have a headache?* I pray that one day he will be able to communicate this with us.

The days do seem to last forever, and over the last four years I haven't gone five minutes without thinking about Luke, past, present, and future. The past is the past. But I miss so much of who we were as a family. I like to savor the memories, but looking at old videos and seeing old pictures on Facebook is so damn hard. I remember the last time I watched Luke play baseball, at a state tournament in Midland, when Luke made amazing defensive plays and had the game-winning hit. I remember the last game we watched together, two nights before the accident, when the Texas Rangers played the Los Angeles Angels. Eventually, they will be fond memories. Today, they are reminders of what I don't have anymore.

The present. My focus moving forward is very simple: Be present and live in the moment. My wife deserves this. And my girls sure do as well. Before I know it, they will both be out of the house. I am so incredibly proud of my three girls. They are blessings beyond blessings (except when their rooms are a mess).

The future. I'm not sure what is worse, thinking about the past, or worrying about the future. *How much better will Luke get? Will I be able to carry him three or five years from now? Will my back give out? What about my girls? Will therapy help them become emotionally secure women? My relationship with Jenny, will we find more joy again?* Jenny and I spent so little time together, just us, over the last three years. I am committed to making our relationship a priority. She's my rock. You see, thinking about the future is just as agonizing. I was never the worrying type. But like I've said, I am not the same person I was before July 28, 2015.

Tim Siegel, 11/12/18

This quote is perfect for me today. I didn't react very well to something today, and it made me think of this. I assume everyone could benefit from reading these words. It reminds me of the pastor, Charles Swindoll, who wrote *Attitude*. My favorite line in that is "Life is 10% what happens to you, and 90% how you react to it." I used to talk about that quote to my team, my family, and anyone who would listen. It was hanging up in my office. But I am guilty of reacting poorly at times in the last 3 years. The severity of the situation shouldn't change how I react. I know that is easier said than done. My least favorite quote of all time is "it is what it is." But the truth is that Luke is the way he is, and I have to make the most of it every single day. For him and for our family. I can't control what's happening, but I certainly can control how I respond to what's happening.

From the early days at UMC and Cook Children's and at every phase of our journey, people have reminded us that God is with us. From nurses and doctors who told us often that, "it's in God's hands" to the words from a stranger at a ball game that "you were chosen for this."

One day, I was thinking about Luke's birthday, April 18, and decided to read the Bible verse Luke 4:18. It reads: "The spirit of the Lord is on me, because he has anointed me to proclaim good news to the poor." I think that this says it all. Luke indeed has been chosen to help others.

A friend said to me recently, "I want you to know that God is using you and Luke in such a powerful way. Don't ever forget that." I won't.

appendix

FAMILIES WE'VE HELPED

The families we support are true inspirations. We love that we get to know them and their children, and watch them progress in their treatments. We love hearing from the families who have been supported through Team Luke Hope for Minds. We receive so many uplifting messages on social media. I receive confirmation every day that I'm doing my best work. Here are some of the wonderful children we helped in our first year. We share these stories on our website, under a section called "Living Proof: Stories of Hope."

Braden suffered an anoxic brain injury after he was shot in the heart with a pellet gun. His family contacted Team Luke Hope for Minds for assistance with hyperbaric oxygen therapy. From Braden's family: "Team Luke Hope for Minds has given us a way to increase our son's potential and to make sure that every therapy possible is available. We can't thank them enough!"

In 2009, Ellie had an aneurysm that hemorrhaged and caused a stroke. As a result, she cannot eat orally, walk, or talk. With support from Team Luke Hope for Minds, Ellie's family was able to buy a handicap accessible van.

Easton suffered a brain injury when he was eight months old. When he was three, his parents reached out to Team Luke Hope for Minds for resources and financial assistance for Easton to receive hyperbaric oxygen therapy with Dr. Paul Harch in New Orleans.

A few days after Lawson was born, he developed some neurological issues possibly due to an infection. Doctors later diagnosed him with a brain injury. Team Luke Hope for Minds helped his family pay for hyperbaric oxygen therapy for Lawson, which has really made a big difference in his recovery.

After Gabe's accident, his therapist suggested his family reach out to Team Luke Hope for Minds. We provided his family with a Lite Gait which helps Gabe with his physical therapy every day.

Alijah suffered a traumatic brain injury in a car accident when he was three years old. His father shared this message about how Team Luke Hope for Minds has helped his family: "I would like to thank Team Luke Hope for Minds for sending my son Alijah Webber to a summer camp for special needs children called CAMP Camp. This is the second year Alijah has attended. Alijah gets to experience things he has never done before, such as horseback riding. When I picked him up from camp, he named every new friend he made at camp. It sure was a long list. I do believe that going to camp is the highlight of the year for Alijah. Thanks again Team Luke Hope for Minds."

Spencer suffered an anoxic brain injury five years ago from a nonfatal drowning while on a family vacation. Team Luke Hope for Minds continues to support him in receiving the best therapy.

George's mom reached out to us seeking assistance for music therapy and therasuit therapy after George developed an anoxic brain injury from a choking incident. We were more than happy to assist. Team Luke Hope for Minds doesn't focus just on the children; we offer financial and educational resources to parents as well. We were excited when George's mom decided to attend our 2017 Pediatric Brain Injury Resource Fair and Conference. She said of the event, "It was great to have so many providers gathered in one place, available for questions and in-depth discussions."

Nalani Davis suffered a brain injury in September 2017, when she was three months old. Team Luke Hope for Minds helped her family purchase a van.

Michael suffered an anoxic brain injury after a nonfatal drowning accident when he was almost two years old. Team Luke Hope for Minds has helped provide neurodevelopmental therapy, a special needs stroller, compression garments, and more. "Team Luke Hope for Minds knows exactly what we're going through," said Michael's mom.

Maddoc was diagnosed with severe hypoxic ischemic encephalopathy, which means his brain did not get sufficient oxygen for several minutes, resulting in brain tissue death. MRI scans showed that almost 100 percent of his brain was damaged. Team Luke Hope for Minds provided financial assistance for two forty-session hyperbaric oxygen therapy treatments. Maddoc's family tells us he is improving slowly but surely. He can smile, coo, and swallow.

Kaden was born with a heart defect that required three corrective surgeries. During his final open-heart surgery, an air embolism went to his brain, causing global brain damage. Team Luke Hope for Minds purchased Kaden a special needs stroller and prism glasses.

After Audrey sustained a traumatic brain injury, Team Luke Hope for Minds provided Audrey's family financial assistance for her to receive hyperbaric oxygen therapy. As a result, she has made positive progress.

Tanner suffered a traumatic brain injury in a car accident. We received this message from Carol, Tanner's mom: "Team Luke Hope for Minds has had a wonderful impact on our son's life. We were introduced to a very helpful yet expensive aid for my son's left hand. Fortunately, we found Team Luke Hope for Minds who graciously provided us with funds towards this amazing aid called Bioness. Because we were able to purchase this product, it also enabled us to have access to an occupational therapist who worked with our son to bring not only improvement to his hand but his left shoulder and arm as well. We continue to see improvement all because Team Luke Hope for Minds helped us access new equipment and therapy for our son. Thank you, Team Luke Hope for Minds!"

Luke suffered an anoxic brain injury from nonfatal drowning in 2017 when he was two years old. Team Luke Hope for Minds helped his family pay for stem cell treatment for Luke.

After Glennabella suffered a global anoxic brain injury, her mother needed assistance paying for hyperbaric oxygen therapy to aid in Glennabella's recovery. Team Luke

Hope for Minds was able to give her family a $5,000 grant for the therapy.

Carter suffered a traumatic brain injury when he was five weeks old. He has spastic quadriplegic cerebral palsy, seizures, cortical vison impairment, and global delays in all areas. "Carter's Law" was adopted in Arkansas in 2013 to educate and raise awareness of shaken baby syndrome.

Bryce suffered a traumatic brain injury from a mountain biking accident. He has made a miraculous recovery and is now attending college at Austin Community College. In his free time, he volunteers for Team Luke Hope for Minds. He loves to visit children who have suffered a brain injury in the hospital and uses his incredible artistic ability to bring joy to the children he visits. Bryce also loves to share his story with the children's parents to bring them hope and encouragement!

Four-year-old Hunter was hospitalized after sustaining a head injury. His family struggled for months to understand how to deal with and support him in the aftermath of a traumatic brain injury. His parents shared the following: "We were relieved when we were introduced to the knowledgeable, kind, and caring 'family' at Team Luke Hope for Minds. Our monthly parent support group introduces speakers on topics that impact the daily lives of our families and offers the opportunity, to share our struggles and successes with understanding supportive people. Had it not been for the recommendations of a number of knowledgeable professional speakers, Hunter would not be on the positive path we are on today. We would never have recognized the array of Hunter's issues as stemming from a TBI. Our family has learned, with the support of Ronda and so many at Team Luke Hope for Minds, where to get professional help with, understand, and deal with Hunter's sadness, aggression, fatigue, and visual issues. We have also learned and will be better prepared for the bumps in the road studies indicate will come during challenging times in Hunter's life."

In October 2016, Nathan suffered a football injury that caused light sensitivity, memory recall issues, an inability to focus, as well as anxiety that led to aggression and depression. Nathan's doctor suggested a lengthy duration of hyperbaric oxygen therapy to help Nathan. We were thrilled to be able to assist them in obtaining an at-home chamber for Nathan to use and are happy to share that he is seeing improvements as a result! Nathan no longer has extreme light sensitivity, he is able to control his emotions better and is improving with his memory and recall. We encourage you to visit our website and watch a video of Nathan talking about his journey, therapy, and what he hopes to do with his life after his memory is fully restored. Also, watch the video of Nathan's mom, Gina, as she talks about how much it means to them to be able to provide Nathan with the therapy he needs to recover!

Chanelle suffered an anoxic brain injury after a non-fatal drowning accident in April 2018. Chanelle's family is hoping and praying that with time and therapy she will be able to live a full life—playing, laughing, and dancing with her siblings. We are thankful we were able to provide financial assistance for stem cell treatment for Chanelle.